*Swim for*

# Swim for Fitness

## MARIANNE BREMS

*With Photographs by Patricia Bresee and David Gray*
*Drawings by Edward J. Patton*

Chronicle Books • San Francisco

**Library of Congress Cataloging in Publication Data**

Brems, Marianne.
    Swim for fitness.

    Bibliography: p. 165
    Includes index.
    1. Swimming.    2. Physical fitness.    I. Title.
GV837.B795        797.2′1        78-32033
ISBN 0-87701-135-4
ISBN 0-87701-124-9 pbk.

Cover photograph by Mark Aronoff

Composition by Hansen & Associates.

**Photo Credits**
Bob Cossins page 13, 73

Chronicle Books
One Hallidie Plaza
San Francisco, CA 94102

# Contents

*To my mother and father,*
*who first took me to the water.*

# Acknowledgements

*I*n reading over the pages I have written, I am humbly grateful to the many individuals whose time and effort have allowed me to present the most complete and up-to-date ideas about swimming and fitness that I possibly can.

First, I most sincerely wish to thank Edward Patton for his drawings, and Patricia Bresee and David Gray for taking the photographs. Also I wish to thank Susan Jones Roy for writing an article specifically for this book.

For taking the time and interest to study my manuscript and record his reaction, I am indebted to Buster Crabbe whose support is a genuine inspiration to me.

For permission to use material not my own I am grateful to James Counsilman, Paul Hutinger, Robert Fuller, Nancy Ridout, and June Krauser. In addition, I received permission from the Amateur Athletic Union of the United States, *Swimming Technique*, World Publications, and the Davis Aquatic Masters.

For consulting with me on various physiological aspects of exercise, I wish to thank Rick Baier, M.D., Harold Dennis, M.D., John Nadeau, M.D., and Patsy Sinnott, R.P.T.

For particular suggestions on improving the manuscript, I owe thanks to Lyn Barretta (to whom I am also indebted for typing my manuscript), to Betty Bennett, to David Levinson, and to David Scott. For film processing, I thank Janet Hagan who coached me in swimming at the Y.M.C.A. when I was thirteen.

And finally, I want to express my gratitude to all the swimmers—particularly the members of the San Mateo Master Marlins—who have made noteworthy comments to me about their sport, and to those enthusiasts, especially Ray and Zada Taft, who from beginning to end wholeheartedly supported my efforts towards creating this book.

# *Why Swim?*

*T*he answer is simple: Swim for fitness. After all, the best preventative measure you can take to guard against dying too soon and enjoying life too little is to achieve and maintain fitness for a lifetime. And it's never too late to start!

But why swim rather than run, or jump, or ride, or swing a racket?

- Because swimming exercises the *entire* body.
- Because swimming can maintain heart rate at a continuously high level.
- Because your blood pressure is lower when you are horizontal than when you are vertical.
- Because your heart volume is significantly greater when you are immersed in water than when you are on land.
- Because water is refreshing and exhilarating.
- Because swimming equipment need not be costly.
- Because water is a better medium than air for exercising weakened or injured muscles.
- Because the risks of injury or heat exhaustion are extremely low.
- Because swimming is so maintainable that you stand an excellent chance of increasing your lifespan.

Swimming, more than any other sport, it's true, exercises the entire body, particularly the shoulders and arms, which are neglected in many sports that involve a great deal of running. And because the human body, unlike other mechanisms, maintains itself and improves its efficiency with *use*; the more of it you can use, the better you will be able to prolong youth and vigor.

And since *continuous* as well as daily use of the body at an increased heart rate is the essence of fitness, the most efficient forms of exercise are those in which a steady pace can be established rather than those which require sudden bursts of energy or very quick movements. For this reason, swimming is an excellent means to fitness, because its rhythmic movements are both steady and efficient.

Blood pressure remains comparatively low during swimming, which is of particular interest to anyone beginning an exercise program after a long period of virtual inactivity, to the older athlete, or to anyone with a tendency toward heart disease. This is partly because of the continuous rather than intermittent nature of swimming, and also because swimming is performed in a horizontal position, so your heart can meet an increased demand for oxygenated blood without having to pump blood directly in opposition to gravity, as in a vertical position.

Important to all swimmers is the fact that—according to the research of Dr. Otto Gauer at the University of Berlin—heart size is greater when you are in a horizontal position than in a vertical one, and greater still when you are immersed in water.[1] What this means to you, the swimmer, is that you are better off than the runner who must combat gravity on two counts. In fact, this increased heart volume can, says Dr. Paul Hutinger, allow you as much as 25 percent more working potential (in terms of how hard you are able to push yourself and how long you can keep going) than a terrestrial athlete who is similar to you in all other ways.

But quite aside from the healthful aspects of swimming, exercising in the water feels good! It massages away minor aches and pains and clears a foggy mind. And most of all, when you swim you escape into a cool silent world where you have only your own motion, your own breathing, and your own thoughts enveloping you in a way that is nothing like life on land. With this, for me, comes exhilaration and a real break in the routine of the day, no matter how unwilling I was initially to get in the water and start.

And swimming equipment is not expensive. All you need is a fast-drying, lightweight bathing suit, a pair of goggles, and, if you choose, a bathing cap, all of which can be purchased for less than $25, a worthwhile investment in your enjoyment and well-being.

The miracle massaging effect of water on muscles and connective tissue weakened by stress, injury, or lack of use is still another reason why swimming meets an exceptionally wide variety of needs. Swimming as an exercise can be as gentle, because of the natural lightness of your body in the water, or as strenuous as you wish.

Similarly, because of your reduced body weight in the water, you do not run the risk of injury in swimming that you do in other sports. For instance, you are not susceptible to jarring pressures on the joints and muscles, and your chances of getting hurt are not, of course, increased by wet weather. You are actually protected in nature's most perfect way —like a baby in the womb. Moreover, because water dissipates the heat of exertion more effectively than air, you run less risk of heat exhaustion than terrestrial athletes and you fatigue less quickly and recover more rapidly.

So there you have it: you can swim even with a tendency toward heart disease or in full health, with an injury or in strength, in wealth or in want, and in good weather or in bad. In short, swimming meets more of the very diverse requirements that people have for exercise than any other sport. And with so many reasons to swim, and so few circumstances to hinder you, swimming can be your uninterrupted personal path to a more enjoyable, vigorous, and quite likely longer life.

Those of you who would like to be part of an organized swimming group will be happy to know that now there is a place for you in the International Masters Swimming Program. The problem with swimming programs until quite recently has been that they were all for teenagers and children, but now adults of any age can swim together in organized groups on a year-round basis for fitness or competition, or both. More detailed information on how to find a program near you is contained in the Appendix.

Training sessions for Masters are held daily and include a mixture of exercises in all four competitive swimming strokes: freestyle, backstroke, breaststroke, and butterfly (though these strokes are not by any means strictly reserved for competition). These sessions also offer instruction in stroke mechanics, and most importantly, include the beginner as well as the advanced swimmer, the slow swimmer as well as the competitor.

Although no age distinction exists in practice sessions, which is one of the beauties of the program, in competition, contestants are divided into age groups by five-year increments, beginning at age twenty-five and going all the way up to the "eighty plus" age division. Many Masters swimmers, however, choose not to compete because the thrill for them comes not from swimming fast, but from swimming regularly at a steady pace with good stroke technique.

Because the Masters swimming program can accommodate the diverse interests, abilities, and ages of swimmers to the end that all can experience a sense of health and well-being while fulfilling personal swimming goals, this program has done so much to make swimming a workable and enjoyable means of achieving and maintaining fitness.

# 1. Finding a Place to Swim

## WHERE CAN I SWIM?

*O*nce you've decided swimming is for you, finding a pool is of primary importance. Other bodies of water may be suitable as well, but if there is a lake or ocean near you I imagine you know about it already.

Probably the most important tool you can use to find out what pool facilities are available in your community is your telephone directory. Check the White Pages for listings under city and county recreation departments, park departments and park districts. Large cities may even show separate swimming or aquatics division numbers. The San Francisco telephone book, for example, has a listing called "Swimming Division Information." Local YMCAs and YWCAs will also be listed in the White Pages, as will colleges, universities, and high schools, which sometimes offer adult fitness swimming sessions for a fee during the early morning or evening hours.

The Yellow Pages of your directory can also be quite useful. The following is a list of headings under which I have found information on swimming:

Athletic Organizations
Clubs
Clubs—Athletic
Recreation Centers
Swimming Clubs
Swimming Instruction
Swimming Pools—Private
Swimming Pools—Public

I have included "Swimming Instruction" in this list because often facilities that are used for teaching can also be used for lap swimming.

But perhaps you have already found a place to swim on your own, and your search is instead for a group to swim with. If this is the case, Appendix A provides a list of Amateur Athletic Union Association offices which have information arranged by state on the Masters Swimming Programs. These offices can refer you to pool locations and provide information about the Masters program. Appendix A is also useful if you plan to travel and you want to find out ahead of time if there is a team with which you can swim in the area to which you will be going.

## SOME DRY FACTS ABOUT SWIMMING FOR NEWCOMERS

### Suits

Choose a suit for practice that is comfortable, snug-fitting, durable, and fast-drying; in short, one that's problem free. One-piece nylon suits best fill this order. (Two-piece suits tend to slip and rub in all the wrong places.) Suits made of lycra (or "skin suits") are popular for competition, because of their skin-hugging quality, but they are relatively expensive and aren't as durable as nylon which makes them less practical for everyday use.

Regardless of its fabric, the best means of prolonging the life of any suit is to avoid sitting on rough surfaces. Rinsing your suit in clear water after every use helps too.

### Caps

The function of a cap is to keep the hair out of your face, not to keep the water out of your hair. Some swimmers use caps in addition to earplugs to keep water out of their ears, however. Like your suit, your cap should be as streamlined as possible. Chin straps can be an obstruction and are often uncomfortable.

### Goggles

Goggles are indispensable when it comes to protecting your eyes from the sting and redness often caused by pool chemicals. Goggles come in different tints to provide maximum comfort in varying degrees of light. You can even choose to see the pool through rose-colored lenses if you wish. But do try goggles of some kind even though you may find that it takes a little time to mold them to your face so they will be watertight.

### Those Lines on the Pool Bottom

Most pools (other than small ones) are equipped with wide, easily visible black lines on the bottom. These are to help you swim straight. They are useful for the obvious reason that the shortest distance between two ends of the pool is a straight line. When many swimmers are in the pool at once, it is a common practice—as well as a common courtesy—to treat each black line as the broken line down the center of a street; the traffic on one side of the line travels single file in one direction, and the traffic on the other side does the same in the opposite direction.

### Sun

The best protection from sun is obviously shade, but since many pools are outdoors (and in them, after all, swimming is at its best) you will probably want to consider taking some steps to protect yourself from sunburn. During your time in the water, a thin coat of ugly-as-anything zinc oxide (sometimes referred to as "clown makeup") will protect your lips, nose or any other vulnerable area without washing off as most sunscreens do. (At least with this one you'll be able to see if it's still on.) Some women prefer lipstick for lip protection.

Most importantly, if your skin is sensitive to the sun, don't spend more time in it than you need to do your swimming. It's the added time you spend in the sun before and after you swim that can cause a problem.

### A Word about Hair

Unless you approach each of your swimming sessions with the attitude that you will be putting your head in the water and that your hair will invariably get wet, you will *not* be able to perform the proper techniques of swimming. But realize, too, that damp curls need not mean that you will lose your fiancé, or whoever, especially when you become healthier and happier and have more self-esteem because of your increased level of fitness. After swimming, you can, of course, always wear a hat or scarf, which keeps the wind out too. And the blow-dry hair styles make the option of drying your hair immediately after swimming attractive.

### Less-than-Lovely Bodies

If you feel that your body fits into this category, remember that no one at the pool cares besides you. As even a cursory glance at this book will reveal to you, your fellow swimmers have enough to think about that unless you have the figure of a fashion model or the physique of a longshoreman, no heads will turn to get a load of how you look in your new tank suit. I have noticed, however, that with the camaraderie that grows between swimmers, most are quick to praise the improvements in appearance of others.

### Between You and You

Keep in mind that how much or how little you swim each day or each week is an issue between you and you. No one else cares as long as you don't get in anyone's way. But here again, I think you will find that your *improvements* in stamina, strength, and technique will be noticed.

## WHAT KINDS OF GOALS ARE SUITABLE FOR ME AND MY SCHEDULE?

When setting goals for yourself, you must remember above all else that maximum cardiovascular fitness ("cardio" meaning "heart" and "vascular" meaning "blood vessels") as well as other physiological benefits, can only be attained through a *regular* program of exercise. Daily training, or at least training three times a week, must be given a high priority when you plan your time, so that swimming doesn't frequently get crowded out of each day's schedule.

Perhaps you feel that this is the hardest part of participating in a fitness swimming program because of the many demands that you feel are being made on your time and energy. But instead, you should think of the time you spend training as an investment toward a long, active, healthy life. And remember that the human body, unlike other mechanisms, functions better with use than with inactivity, and a healthy body will perform more efficiently and yield greater joy in all aspects of life.

As far as setting specific goals for yourself, perhaps a look at your own personal progress will prove more helpful than anything else. My assumption is that you will want to just plain swim for awhile to get used to the whole idea of jumping in the water every day and boosting your heart rate before you set any goals beyond firming up, or making friends, or doing what your doctor suggested. Remember, you have a lifetime to swim and set goals if you wish. But, if you make observations as to your heart rate (see Chapter 2 to learn how heart rate can be a guide) and the time or distance you can swim without exhaustion when you begin your training, and you continue to monitor this information,

you will be able to notice your progress almost immediately.

If you find that your body adapts rapidly to increasing amounts of stress and that you don't feel tired the rest of the day from your efforts at the pool, then you may find stimulation in swimming against the clock and decreasing your rest intervals and increasing your distances. Perhaps you will even want to consider swimming in competition once you have learned the basic techniques necessary for swimming in a meet.

Many swimmers, however, have no interest at all in competition. Their goals may range from wanting to strengthen the abdominal muscles that have been strained during pregnancy, wanting to loosen connective tissues in areas of the body that have suffered injury, or wanting to make a particular swim, as Dr. Joyce Brothers did when she swam the distance from New York to Princeton. One day she decided to add novelty to her daily routine at the pool by swimming, a small portion at a time, the equivalent distance from her apartment to her daughter's college. She pinned a road map on the wall of her study and she marked off her progress every day until she had completed the 53 mile distance.[2]

But all swimmers, no matter what their personal goals (and they must indeed be personal to be of any value), will be better able to set goals if they have an understanding of the types of training and training techniques described in

Chapter 7.

Certainly it bears repeating, though, that training must be *regular*. For this reason, most Masters workouts and adult swim sessions are scheduled, based on pool availability, to meet the time needs of the greatest number of swimmers— namely, early mornings, noon hours, and evenings. You may find that because of your personal metabolism rate, which varies throughout the day, you swim better at one time of the day than at another, so experiment if possible. And once you are over the initial adjustment period of starting a daily swimming program, try to swim for approximately the same length of time each day so that your body establishes a routine. It is not advisable to try to make up for missed practices by swimming twice as long the following day. You would benefit far more from doing some strength and flexibility exercises such as those described in Chapter 10 on days that you do not swim.

## HAVING A PHYSICAL EXAMINATION

It is a good idea for any adult who wishes to swim either for general fitness and well-being or in competition to have a complete physical examination before attempting to set goals for himself or herself. But to avoid paying too much for an examination which reveals too little, it is just as important that you find a doctor to administer the exam who has a full understanding of physical fitness and who preferably is active in some sport himself, as Hal Higdon[3] says. The doctor should at least be aware of both the many physiological changes the body undergoes as a result of exercise and the major role that a regular fitness program necessarily plays in an individual's life. In many cases, it is inappropriate for a doctor to take the simplified, overly cautious approach and say to an athlete that because he has a headache or an earache he must stay out of the water for three weeks, for example. This is not to say that potentially serious ailments should not be given serious attention, but sometimes doctors who are not sports doctors overlook the fact that if a participant totally abstains from his regular program of physical activity, it can be very distressing for him, not only mentally, but physically as well, since muscle atrophy begins after as little as sixty hours of inactivity.

So in order that you receive the right tests, properly administered, and get medical advice as to how the results of your physical examination relate specifically to the activity of swimming, find a doctor who understands the special needs of an athlete. Such a doctor can usually be found by inquiring at large hospitals over the telephone.

According to Dr. Paul Hutinger, professor of physical

education at Western Illinois University and a Masters swimmer, the tests which should be included in a meaningful physical examination are a complete blood test, a urinalysis, a pulse check, a blood pressure test, and an *exercise* electrocardiogram, as indicators of your general condition.[4] The standard resting electrocardiogram, it should be noted, reveals little about the condition of the working heart. The exercise electrocardiogram (EKG stress test) will, on the other hand, show the heart's stroke volume and functional abilities which decrease with age but also increase with regular exercise. In addition, the EKG stress test can help to relieve any apprehensions that a well-trained adult might have concerning high heart rates incurred during training, by showing that the heart which is accustomed to exercise can handle a heavy work load with a relatively low heart rate because of its large stroke volume.[5]

To take an EKG stress test, a treadmill or bicycle ergometer (stationary bicycle) is the best device because each allows the body to reach its maximum capacity rapidly. The Harvard Step Test, which requires only a bench and is therefore more readily available, may also be used, but it takes much longer. As far as finding out where you can obtain an EKG stress test, contact your local Heart Association or your physician.[6] Also, large colleges and universities sometimes have sports physiology labs that are equipped to administer such tests.

But having your doctor make a thorough analysis and evaluation of any past medical problems you may have had is just as important as taking all the proper tests when you have a physical examination. For example, anyone who has suffered back trouble may find that the dolphin kick used in butterfly can irritate the lower back and should therefore be avoided, or a heart valve problem could shunt the blood flow from the heart to the body.

## CHAPTER SUMMARY

### Where Can I Swim?

To find a pool check the white pages of your phone book under: city recreation departments, county recreation departments, park departments, park districts, YMCAs, YWCAs, and schools.
Look in the yellow pages under: Athletic Organizations, Clubs, Clubs—Athletic, Recreation Centers, Swimming Clubs, Swimming Instruction, Swimming Pools—Private, and Swimming Pools—Public.
If you want to find a Masters group to swim with, check Appendix A.

### Some Dry Facts about Swimming for Newcomers

1. Suits.
2. Caps.
3. Goggles.
4. Those lines on the bottom.
5. Sun.
6. A word about hair.
7. Less-than-lovely bodies.
8. Between you and you.

### What Kind of Goals are Suitable for Me and My Schedule?

Maximum physiological benefits can only be attained through a regular program of exercise. So look at the time you spend training as an investment toward a long, active, healthy life rather than as an intrusion on your daily schedule.

### Having a Physical Examination

Before beginning a well-planned and regular program of fitness you should have a physical examination by a physician who understands and preferably participates in sports.

The examination should include the following:

1. Blood test.
2. Urinalysis.
3. Pulse check.
4. Blood pressure test.
5. Exercise EKG.
6. Review and analysis of any past medical problems you have had.

# 2. *Getting Ready*

## HOW MUCH SWIMMING SHOULD I DO TO START?

*B*efore even entering the water, you should think about your present physical condition. Have you ever followed a regular program of exercise for more than three weeks? Have you participated in any daily or weekly physical activity program in the past year? Are you the occasional-game-of tennis or seasonal-hike-in-the-woods kind of sports enthusiast? Do you engage in any other type of activity three or more times per week which contributes to cardiovascular fitness, such as running, rowing, or cycling? Did you compete in sports as a teenager or in college, and did you maintain a minimum level of fitness afterward? Answering these questions and others like them will provide you with a starting point from which to roughly determine how soon you will fatigue in the water. But, of course, to truly gauge your present condition you must get into the pool.

Once you find yourself immersed in water, your first attempts to glide smoothly and effortlessly down the pool may make you wonder if your Aunt Agatha wasn't right when she said swimming might put a dangerous strain on your heart. In fact, you should check your heart rate in beats per minute several times during the first 5 to 10 minutes. To determine your heart rate while in the pool, check your pulse over your heart for ten seconds as soon as you have completed the last length of a swim, then multiply by 6 to give the total number of beats per minute. (For this you can use your own wrist watch if nothing else is available; however, many pools have large pace clocks that are easy to read from a distance.) In doing so, you can relieve any apprehensions you might have for your safety by simply keeping your heart rate (as taken immediately after completing a particular swim) at a level not to exceed 60 percent of the difference between your resting heart rate (as taken before you rise from bed in the morning) and your maximum heart rate, according to Herbert A. deVries.[7]

To figure your maximum heart rate, a standard formula you can use is to subtract your age from 220, which is considered to be the theoretical maximum heart rate. For example, if you are 40 years old, you would subtract 40 from 220 to give a maximum heart rate of 180. You can also use Table 2.1 as a guide.

### Table 2.1 MAXIMUM HEART RATE AND AGE[8]

| Age | Maximum Heart Rate |
|-----|--------------------|
| 20 years old | 200-220 bpm |
| 30 years old | 190-200 bpm |
| 40 years old | 180-190 bpm |
| 50 years old | 170-180 bpm |
| 60 years old | 160-170 bpm |
| 70 years old | 150-160 bpm |

Reprinted with permission from World Publications, P.O. Box 366, Mountain View, Ca. 94042.

So, to figure 60 percent of the difference between your resting and your maximum heart rate you would proceed as follows:

220 minus your age = A
A minus your resting heart rate = B
B times 60% = C
C plus your resting heart rate = safe heartbeat for exercise.

For example:

| | |
|---|---|
| 220 | (theoretical maximum heart rate) |
| −40 | (age) |
| 180 | |
| −70 | (resting heart rate) |
| 110 | |
| ×.60 | (60%) |
| 66 | |
| +70 | (resting heart rate) |
| 136 | (60% of the difference between resting and maximum heart rates) |

In general, caution must accompany your enthusiasm when you begin a training program. If you can swim 50 meters without reaching an excessive heart rate level, which would be more than 60 percent of the difference between your resting and your maximum heart rate, then try for 100 meters or 150, and so forth. Choose a work load that you can handle without exhaustion. After all, remember that your purpose is to maintain fitness and to swim for a lifetime which cannot be accomplished under the drudgery of exhaustion.

So you must pace yourself. Take the I-have-plenty-of-time approach. Swim at a moderate heart rate for 12 to 20 minutes per session for the first few weeks, or until you begin to notice a drop in heart rate or an increase in the distance you can swim without excessive fatigue. And swim only three or four times a week for the first month rather than every day because soreness sometimes takes 36 hours or more to occur and you don't want to overdo it. Also, change strokes often if you can do more than one stroke. This will help you to develop the full range of motion necessary for efficient swimming while avoiding strain and minimizing fatigue. And for at least the first three weeks, don't watch the pace clock except to check your pulse; instead do only a designated number of laps at your own pace.

As a final check that your pace is right for you, monitor your resting heart rate before practice, then for the first week or so, check again after you return home from swimming. After a few sessions in the water the two heart rates should be fairly close even if the work load is strenuous, but not excessive.

It should, however, be mentioned here that although many adults enter the Masters swimming program after a long period of physical inactivity or with no previous experience in a fitness program, some begin at a relatively high level of conditioning. Such swimmers must train more vigorously and for longer periods of time each day than the beginner in order to maintain cardiovascular fitness and strength. Well-conditioned Masters swimmers interested in achieving maximum performance or who are interested in competition often do 1000–2000 meters or more a day of mostly high quality swimming five or even six days a week. (Detailed training methods for high quality swimming are given in Chapter 7.) This usually results in good times for events ranging from 50 to 200 meters. If success in longer events is what you want, however, you should increase your daily distance to 3000 or even 5000 meters a day during specific peak periods or seasons when you are training for some particular event or events. But I would not recommend that you train more distance per day on a year-round basis than you can do in one hour. With hard training as with hard work of any kind, you need to intersperse some weeks or even months of shorter training sessions between any extended periods of long training each day.

Some Masters swimmers, who perhaps have more time to train than the average adult, have been successful and satisfied with swimming two or even three hours a day. But the tendency for most adult swimmers is to "burn out" or grow tired in such a situation, and thus to lose sight of the idea of swimming for a lifetime.

## HOW OFTEN SHOULD I SWIM?

Changes in muscle tone and cardiovascular capacity are brought about only by exerting the body beyond what it is used to so that it must adapt to an increased demand for blood and oxygen. Also, the greater the extent to which the body has already adapted, the greater the exertion required to make it adapt still further. This means that a body that has already attained a relatively high level of fitness requires more frequent stress than a body that is just beginning, which is why Olympians swim two or even three times a day. The beginner, too, has the consideration that if he tries to firm up or slim down too quickly, he may do initial damage which will only serve to slow down the process. But a few general rules apply to both the beginner and the more advanced swimmer.

First, it is important to remember, as mentioned earlier, that muscle atrophy or deterioration of muscle tone can begin after as little as 60 hours. This means that in order to bring about any lasting changes in muscle tone or to maintain a minimal level of muscular strength and endurance, you must exercise at least every other day, or three times a week. The same minimum standard is also applicable to your cardiovascular capacity and to your body's level of ability to absorb oxygen that is inhaled (aerobic fitness).

But the length and the intensity of these sessions must also meet a minimum standard. Each period of swimming should be at least one half hour long, allowing approximately 10 minutes for warm-up, and moderate swimming, using different strokes so that the muscles will be prepared for more intense swimming, 12 to 20 minutes for swimming at more than 60 percent (depending upon your condition and your goals) of your maximum heart rate, and up to 5 minutes of easy swimming (a "swim-down") to relieve the buildup in the body of waste products such as lactic acid, which can cause muscle soreness (a hot shower also helps). As the body adapts to the increased demands for blood and oxygen during exercise, the 12 to 20 minute period of stress swimming will have to be increased, but this should most certainly be in addition to, and not at the expense of, the warmup and swim-down. You should include a warmup and a swim-down in every swimming session no matter what your physical condition and the content of your workout.

Second, it is important to remember that the body at any level of physical conditioning and at any age thrives on regular use. It is never too late to start, even if you are the victim of a heart attack, and you will never be too old to maintain the body you have built. In fact, the aging process on many of your physiological mechanisms can be greatly slowed or even reversed (examples of this can be found in Appendix C) through a regular program of swimming from three times a week to eight or nine hours a week depending upon your age, ability, and goals.

## HOW HARD SHOULD I PUSH MYSELF?

The most important factor in determining how hard to push yourself during a swimming session is heart rate. This provides the most exact means of determining just where you stand in relation to your present physical capabilities, whether you are a beginner or an experienced, well-conditioned swimmer. Figuring your maximum heart rate, then monitoring your heart rate just after high stress swimming, during recovery from high stress, and during complete rest can tell you at what percentage of your maximum output you have been swimming, how much rest to take between swims, and when you should take a day off from swimming.

To figure your maximum heart rate a stress test on a treadmill or bicycle ergometer is best, but you can, for convenience, subtract your age from 220, or use Table 2.1 Once you establish your maximum, then if you check your pulse (count for 6 seconds and multiply by 10 to get your heart rate for 1 minute) immediately after a hard swimming series, such as 10 × 50 meters or 10 × 100 meters, or one very hard swim and subtract the result from your maximum, you can figure at what percentage of your maximum you just swam. For example, if after a hard effort you have a heart rate of 18 beats for 6 seconds, then your heart rate for 1 minute would be 180 beats; if your maximum heart rate is 200 then your effort was at 90 percent of your maximum. Depending upon your level of conditioning and your goals, you will want to do the stress portion of your training session at 60 to 90 percent of your maximum heart rate.

But you must be aware of your recovery rate, as well. This varies greatly from person to person, and it also depends on the length of time that the heart was operating at a high capacity. According to *Aquatic World*, Jenny Turall, a world class distance swimmer, can recover from a 400 meter swim at 90 percent of her capacity with a pulse rate of 168 to one of 60 in 30 seconds and to a rate of 48 in 1 minute. Another swimmer, on the other hand, might take 10 minutes or more to recover from such an effort.[9]

In any case, the higher your level of fitness, the closer you will be able to train to your maximum heart rate and the more consecutive minutes you will be able to maintain a high heart rate. You should, however, check your heart rate every 10 minutes or so, not only immediately after a hard swimming series (swims of equal distance with short rest in between, such as 10 × 50 meters or 10 × 100 meters), but also 30 seconds after, 1 minute after, 2 minutes after, and so on or until your heart rate is below 100. If your heart rate drops 40 to 50 beats per minute or more during the first minute, you have achieved a high level of fitness. If your heart rate does not drop to 100 or less in 3 minutes, however, then you should take a longer rest between swims in a series. How much additional rest you need you will have to judge for yourself, but use heart rate as your guide. Give yourself enough rest so that with some effort you can maintain a fairly constant time for all of the swims in a 25, 50, 100 meter, or any distance series, but do not rest so long between swims in a series that your pulse rate drops more than 40 to 60 beats per minute below your stress rate.

Another statistic you should keep on yourself is your basal or lowest resting heart rate. This should be taken as soon as you wake up in the morning and *before* you rise from bed. If you then find that you remain tired long after practice is over for the day, take your pulse the next morning and if it is ten or more beats per minute above your normal, you might do well to take the day off from swimming. It is also a good idea to check your heart rate occasionally when you come home from the pool, especially if you are feeling more tired than usual. Your pulse should be within ten beats of your basal heart rate if you are healthy, reasonably rested, and your work load in the pool is compatible with your physical condition.

But you should also be aware, quite aside from any figures, of how you *feel*. For example, if your arms feel heavy from hard swimming the day before, it might be appropriate for you to forget about the clock and heart rate for a day or two and just concentrate on stroke or a designated distance.

A coach or supervisor of a swimming group can also be helpful. This person can tell unsuspecting swimmers if they are leaning too long on one arm to breathe, which can cause tendonitis, or if they are demonstrating other signs of fatigue.

## SOME MEANS OF ASSESSING PERSONAL PROGRESS

The joyous sensation of discovering that you have made progress since you began swimming may well do more toward making you want to continue than all the advice and suggestions in this book. So do not miss the opportunity to evaluate your progress. To do this, you may want to make some notes on the various aspects of where you stand with your swimming at the present so that in the weeks, months, or years to come you can compare data.

The most obvious and simple way to observe improvement in your fitness level is either to look at the time it takes you to do a given distance now, as compared with some point in the past, or to measure how much farther you can swim now in a given time than before. Another good indicator of adaptation to the stress of swimming is being able to hold an even pace over a long distance, or over a number of shorter swims with only a short rest in between (a series). If you learn to do this well, then you will also be able to predict your times for distances you have not yet swum, which can be very satisfying.

As your strength and endurance grow and you are increasing your number of laps per session, you might enjoy keeping track of the number of miles you do, as Dr. Joyce Brothers did when she decided to swim the equivalent distance from New York to Princeton.

You can also discover improvement in your stroke efficiency by counting the number of strokes it takes you to complete one length of the pool and comparing this with performances at other times. But be careful that in your effort to improve you do not stop your arm motion at some point during the stroke and thereby come up with a misrepresentative total. Counting strokes is also a useful device in learning to maintain stroke efficiency. For example, you can try to do 50 meters, or 100 meters, or any distance of more than one length, making an effort to maintain the same number of strokes on each length. The farther you swim, of course, and the more tired you become, the more difficult it is to maintain a constant number of strokes.

Adapting to taking more strokes without breathing is another sign of improvement — improvement in your body's level of ability to use oxygen already in the body (anaerobic capacity), a necessary adaptation for short, fast swims.

Faster recovery heart rates also demonstrate an improvement in cardiovascular fitness, as does your ability to repeat more swims in a series in a given interval (see section on interval training in Chapter 7). Both are related to the fact that the trained heart can accept a greater work load with a lower heart rate than the untrained heart because heart stroke volume increases with physical stress.

But quite aside from the thrill you will experience, or perhaps already have experienced from observing right in the pool the previously mentioned changes in your own physiology, you will also find if you were to take a few out-of-the-water tests such as those in Appendix C that many other beneficial "anti-aging" processes are taking place in your body.

# CHAPTER SUMMARY

## How Much Swimming Should I Do to Start?

Begin by swimming a moderate amount and take your time increasing your distance if you are new to swimming or if you have been away from it for some time. Remember you have a lifetime to swim.

Figure your maximum heart rate and do not swim longer than the length of time for which you can stay at or below 60 percent of the difference between your resting and your maximum heart rate.

If you are just beginning, swim for 12 to 20 minutes per session at least three times a week for the first week, or until you begin to notice a drop in your working heart rate. If you are experienced and in good condition, and you are interested in competing with the best, you should swim five or six days a week, if possible, doing from 1000 to 2000 meters per day, or up to 5000 meters per day if you wish to specialize in long events.

## How Often Should I Swim?

Swim a minimum of three times per week. If you have the time and inclination, swim more often, for this will improve your proficiency as well as your level of fitness.

## How Hard Should I Push Myself?

Heart rate is the key to determining how hard to push yourself.

Depending upon your level of conditioning, the stress portion of your training session should be done at 60 to 90 percent of your maximum heart rate.

Be aware of your recovery heart rate so you will know how much rest to take between swims.

Establish your basal heart rate before rising from bed in the morning and check each morning to see that your heart rate is not higher than normal.

Stay in touch with how you feel so that you do not push yourself to the point that swimming becomes an exhausting drudgery.

## Some Means of Assessing Personal Progress

1. Swimming as far as you can in a given time and comparing this distance with the distance you swim in the same time at some future point.
2. Timing yourself for a given distance and comparing this time with your time for the same distance done at some future point.
3. Gaining the ability to do swims in a series holding a constant time for each swim.
4. Charting your mileage.

5. Improving your stroke efficiency so that you reduce the number of strokes you need to swim each length.

6. \ Increasing the number of swims you can repeat on a given interval.

# 3. Freestyle: The Most Efficient Stroke in Swimming

*F*reestyle is the most efficient stroke in swimming. For this reason, you will probably swim more of it than anything else, because swimming a high number of yards in a short period of time will be essential during much of your training time.

After some deliberation I decided to use the term "freestyle" to describe the stroke that the American Red Cross and other organizations call the "crawl stroke." I based this decision on my observation that purely instructional swimming programs most often use the term "crawl stroke," whereas long range programs that stress training along with stroke instruction usually use the term "freestyle." Freestyle also is applied in competition swimming when the stroke used is at the discretion of the individual swimmer. The stroke nearly always chosen, however, is the crawl stroke, because almost everyone finds it to be the most efficient and therefore the fastest swimming stroke.

In freestyle, as in the other strokes, you move forward not by moving water backward, as is sometimes thought, but by pushing the arms and legs against the resistance offered by the water. When you thrust against the water with your hand, the water offers resistance against your hand, moving you forward — simple application of Newton's Third Law of Motion, that for every action there is an equal and opposite reaction. In other words, you push your body past your hand just as you do if you take a step with a pair of crutches by placing them firmly on the floor and swinging your body past your arms.

But the floor is solid, you may say, and the water is nothing more than a billion moving molecules that offer little stability. Take heart, things aren't as shaky as you think, because someone was thinking of you when modern stroke mechanics were devised. This isn't to say that I am about to divulge the secret of walking on water, but I would like to show you a way to constantly push your hands against the stillest possible water so that you will have the best "hold" on it and can thereby push yourself forward with maximum efficiency. (Bear in mind, however, that no one stroke technique is completely correct for *every* person and that within the limits of the following principles, you must find the method that is best for you.)

## UNDERWATER ARM PULL

Clearly, if you can press your hand against water that is not moving, you can push yourself further forward than if you are in water that is already moving backward. So, when pushing against still water, you should make an elongated

"S" pattern (see Figure 3.1) with your hands when you swim freestyle. This way your hand will avoid following a column of water that is moving from the moment you begin your pull backwards.

As you can see in Figure 3.1, the hand zigzags back and forth so that it may constantly encounter still water, which will offer the greatest resistance. (Notice, however, that the hand does not move all the way across the body.)

You will also observe in Figure 3.2 that the arm is bent significantly throughout the major portion of the pull. The reason for this is that leverage is greatest with a bent arm.

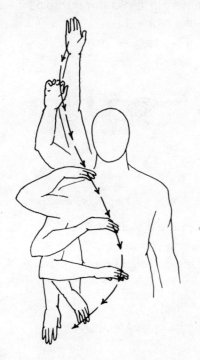

Figure 3.1   **Underwater elongated "S" pull pattern**

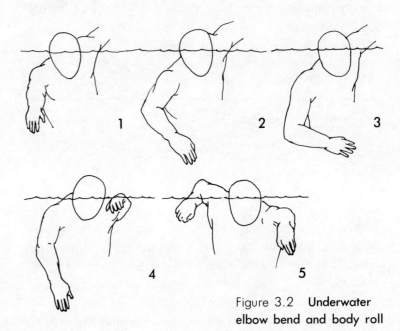

Figure 3.2   **Underwater elbow bend and body roll**

You can see this principle at work when you try to lift your body out of the pool by placing your hands on top of the pool wall and pressing downward. You will naturally bring your body in as close to the wall as possible and bend your elbows for the initial thrust, rather than standing back from the wall and attempting the feat with straight arms.

But as you bend your elbow to pull backward, be sure that your elbow remains high above your hand as in Figure 3.3 because this will allow you the greatest possible surface with which to push against the water.

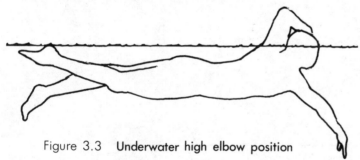

Figure 3.3   **Underwater high elbow position**

You should, however, fully extend each arm, letting your body roll, just after your hand enters the water in front and just before it leaves the water at the end of the stroke. This way you will be able to get the greatest distance per stroke, which is the key to maximum efficiency.

The angle or "pitch" at which the hands enter the water is also important when considering resistance and efficiency (Fig. 3.4). The hand shouldn't entrap air as it enters, because if it does the resistance against which the hand pushes to move the body ahead will be decreased, making the stroke less efficient. To avoid air entrapment you must knife each hand into the water thumb-first, with the palm forming approximately a 45-degree angle with the surface of the water, as in Figure 3.4.

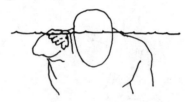

Figure 3.4   **Angle of hand entry**

The hands also should knife out of the water at the end of the arm pull to facilitate an easy arm recovery. As it leaves the water each hand should be perpendicular to the surface, with the little finger leaving the water first, as in Figure 3.5.

## ARM RECOVERY

When I use the term "arm recovery" I refer strictly to the out-

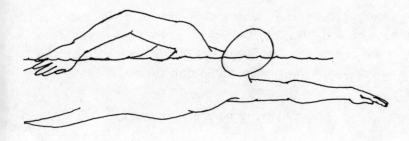

Figure 3.5 **Angle of hand at exit**

of-water portion of the stroke — although some coaches believe that the recovery actually begins before the hand and forearm leave the water. What essentially happens in the arm recovery is that the elbow comes up above the head and swings forward with the forearm relaxed (see Figure 3.6).

Once the elbow swings forward, the hand then enters the water in front of the shoulder, as you can see in Figures 3.5 and 3.6.

The kicking portion of freestyle is the "flutter" kick, an up-and-down leg beat. The key to effective flutter kicking is ankle flexibility. The reason for this is that the more fully you can extend your ankles, the greater the surface area of the foot will be able to push against the water forcing the body forward. (Your feet are acting as "swim fins" in this motion.) The knees bend slightly on the downbeat but are kept straight on the upbeat, as in Figure 3.7. The distance between the feet when they are furthest apart should be about 12 to 16 inches (about 30 to 45 cm.).

When doing the freestyle, many swimmers use a six-beat kick — six downward kicks (three with each foot) for every complete arm cycle (right and left arms). Some swimmers, however, prefer the two-beat kick, with only two downward kicks (one with each foot) for every complete arm cycle. The best way to decide which kick is best for you is simply to do the one that comes naturally and stick with that rhythm.

1    2    3

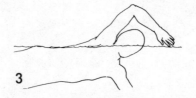

Figure 3.6 **Out-of-water arm recovery**

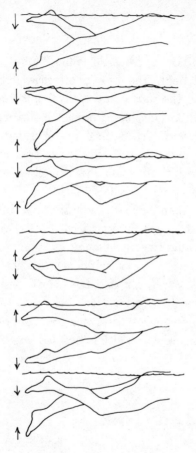

Figure 3.7 **Kick**

Don't worry if other swimmers around you prefer the other type of kick. Also, don't worry about the timing; one of the great beauties of the flutter kick is that each beat falls in naturally with the rhythm of the arm stroke.

## BODY POSITION AND BREATHING

When considering body position (see Figure 3.8), you should realize that streamlining is of utmost importance (unless, of course, you deliberately want to create resistance for the purpose of building strength in training). For maximum efficiency when swimming freestyle, your body position must be such that the legs do not sag significantly below the level of the shoulders and your feet should not be more than 12 to 16 inches (about 30 to 45 cm.) below the surface. The heel of the higher foot should break the surface when the other foot is at its lowest point.

Figure 3.8 **Body position**

In order to achieve this position, you must hold your head so that the water line falls at about your hairline. If the head is held too high the feet will drop too low and consequently increase resistance.

Also, notice in Figure 3.8 that as the right arm fully extends in front of the body, the left arm extends to the rear.

## BREATHING

Breathing is often the most worrisome aspect of swimming freestyle. Many swimmers have learned improper breathing techniques or have simply gotten a mouthful of water once too often, which leaves them reluctant to keep working at breathing until it becomes an easy and natural part of their stroke.

You can breathe on either the right side or the left side; inhalation should occur with the head turned to the side like a doorknob — not lifted out of the water—just as the hand on the same side leaves the water to begin recovery. You don't have to turn your head too far to the side or lift it up to breathe since the head, as it moves through the water, creates a wave, the back side of which is an air pocket suitable for breathing (Figure 3.9).

Figure 3.9 **Inhalation phase of breathing**

After taking a breath your head returns at once to its face down position, as in Figure 3.10. And, depending upon whether you are breathing every stroke or less often, you will either exhale very slowly or very quickly in this face-down position (Fig. 3.10). In either case, you must be sure that your breath is expelled *completely* before turning your head again to inhale. If you do not exhale completely, a mistake that is easy to make but difficult for a coach or observer to detect, you will find that you fatigue very quickly.

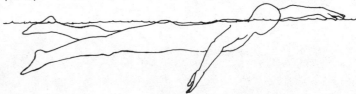

Figure 3.10 **Exhalation phase of breathing**

Once you have mastered the breathing technique, it's a

good idea to learn to breathe on either side. This way, during training you can alternate breathing first on your right side and then on your left side and so on, which will balance your stroke. A balanced stroke is one in which the right side of your body performs the same motions in the same positions as the left side of your body. Sometimes when breathing is limited to one side only, the arm pull, the kick, or the roll of the body as one arm extends forward may be slightly different on one side than on the other.

## SOME COMMON STROKE DEFECTS

### Arms

1.   Hand or hands pull too far across the body on the underwater pull (Fig. 3.11). This causes the body to roll too far distorting the body position.

Figure 3.11   **Hand crossing over too far**

2.   Lifting the hands out of the water before they pass the hips (Fig. 3.12). This greatly reduces the distance per stroke because the arm has the greatest pushing power at the end of the stroke.

Figure 3.12   **Lifting hand too soon**

3.   Making too wide an arm recovery (Fig. 3.13). This tends to push the head and upper body to one side causing the stroke to be constantly pushed out of alignment.

Figure 3.13   **Wide arm recovery**

4.   Carrying hands too high during arm recovery (Fig. 3.14). Most importantly, this requires more energy than carrying the hand close to the surface. Also, this movement tends to push the upper body slightly lower in the water, causing unnecessary resistance.

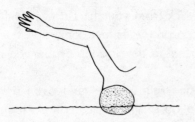

Figure 3.14 **High hand during recovery**

### Legs

1. Keeping the ankles too stiff (not allowing full extension). This greatly reduces the surface of the foot which can push against the water and thereby decreases the efficiency of the kick.

2. Kicking too deeply (Fig. 3.15). This causes the body to sit at an angle in the water, which creates unnecessary resistance. Also, a kick that is too deep can throw off the timing of the arm stroke.

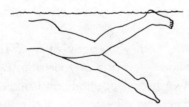

Figure 3.15 **Kicking too deeply**

3. Kicking from the knees only (Fig. 3.16). This will exclude the use of the large thigh muscles. The motion of a proper kick should begin at the hip and include the entire leg for maximum strength.

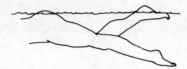

Figure 3.16 **Kicking from the knees**

### Breathing

1. Holding the head too high (Fig. 3.17). This causes the legs and lower body to move too low in the water. It's also more difficult to make a proper arm recovery when the shoulders are lower.

Figure 3.17 **Head too high**

2. Lifting the head to breathe. This pushes the legs and lower body down in the water just as does holding the head too high.

3. Turning the whole body to breathe rather than only the head. This requires too much energy and also distorts body position.

## FREESTYLE STROKE DRILLS

Through a combination of imagination, observing the practice sessions of other coaches and studying a series of drills compiled by coach Dick Hannula[10] I have arrived at the following list of freestyle exercises. (I used the same method to devise the exercises for the other strokes.)

### Legs:

1. Sit as close to the edge of the pool as possible, dangling your legs in the water. Kick your feet slowly up and down with ankles as loose as possible. *Purpose:* to get the feel of the water pressing your toes down during propulsion.
2. Repeat drill 1 above using swim fins (see Chapter 7 under "Training Devices"). *Purpose:* to exaggerate the feel of the water pressing your toes down during propulsion.
3. Extend your body on the surface, stomach down, holding onto the gutter or pool wall with one hand and placing your other hand flat against the wall 2 feet below the surface. Freestyle kick from your hips down so that your heels break the surface and your feet come apart vertically 12 to 16 inches. *Purpose:* to develop the proper technique with no distractions.
4. Freestyle kick with arms extended on a kickboard. (A detailed description of this device can be found in Chapter 7.) *Purpose:* to build strength and endurance into your kick.
5. Freestyle kick with arms extended, no kickboard, face in the water. *Purpose:* to streamline your body position.
6. Freestyle kick with arms extended forward, your body underwater. *Purpose:* to improve your feel for the ankle and leg motions.
7. Freestyle kick, on your side, bottom arm extended near the surface, top arm at your side. Practice on both sides. *Purpose:* to make it possible to observe the width and depth of your kick.
8. Freestyle kick with your body at a 45-degree angle, bottom arm extended, top arm at your side. Practice on both sides. *Purpose:* to simulate crawl stroking position during kicking.
9. Freestyle kick, with your body at a 45-degree angle, bottom arm extended, top arm at your side. Do six kicks on one side, then switch arm positions and angle, and do six kicks on the other side. Repeat for the desired distance. *Purpose:* to work on a six-beat kick suitable for proper

stroking rhythm and to improve the length of your arm extension.

10.  Freestyle kick with your body at a 45-degree angle, bottom arm extended, top arm at side. Do three kicks on one side, then three kicks on the other side as in drill 9. *Purpose*: to simulate the six-beat kick used when stroking, and to improve arm extension.

You may do any of these drills with swim fins to develop feel and to add variety.

### Arms and Whole Stroke

1.  Hold a kickboard in the middle of the bottom edge with one hand, stroke with your other arm placing your finger tips just under the bottom edge of the board and directly in front of your shoulders. Repeat, switching hand positions. *Purpose*: to work on the proper entry position for your hands and to prevent them from crossing over too far in front of your body.
2.  Freestyle with one arm, other arm extended in front. *Purpose*: to practice hand entry.
3.  Freestyle, dragging fingertips through the water on the recovery. *Purpose*: to get the elbows up high on recovery phase.
4.  Count the number of arm strokes needed to swim one

length of the pool. Repeat, trying to extend your arms in the forward and backward positions as much as possible but keeping the arms constantly moving, and attempt to reduce the number of strokes required to swim one length. *Purpose*: to learn to gain as much distance per stroke as possible.
5.  Freestyle, breathing alternately on one side and then on the other. *Purpose*: to gain stroke balance.
6.  "Dog paddle" or human stroke with exaggerated roll. *Purpose*: to develop the body roll necessary for proper stroke technique.
7.  Freestyle with one arm, other arm at side. Practice on both sides. *Purpose*: to promote a rapid turnover, a fast hand entry, and a rapid kick.
8.  Freestyle with fists. *Purpose*: to demonstrate the importance of creating resistance when pressing against the water.
9.  Freestyle with arms only, a pull buoy (a detailed description of this device can be found in Chapter 7) or other flotation device attached to your legs. *Purpose*: to work on your arm pull without distractions, and to streamline your body position.
10.  Freestyle with arms only, a pull buoy between your legs, and a small (see Chapter 7 under "Resistance Devices") innertube around your feet. *Purpose*: same as drill 9 but more resistance.

You may do any of the above drills with hand paddles to increase resistance and to add variety. You should, however, exercise caution to see that undue soreness does not develop with the increased strain of adding more resistance.

## CHAPTER SUMMARY:

The term "freestyle" is used to mean the same as "crawl stroke." Newton's Third Law of Motion, which states that for every action there is an equal and opposite reaction, is directly applicable to the technique of swimming.

### Underwater Arm Pull

1. Elongated "S" pull pattern.
2. Body roll and elbow bend.
3. High elbow.
4. Arm extension for maximum distance per stroke.
5. Hand entry at 45-degree angle.
6. Hand exit perpendicular to the surface.

### Arm Recovery

1. High elbow.
2. Hand entry in front of the shoulder.

### Kick

1. Ankle extension.
2. Slight knee bend on downbeat.
3. Straight knee on upbeat.
4. Depth of kick 12 to 16 inches (about 30 to 45 cm.).
5. Six-beat kick.
6. Two-beat kick.

### Body Position and Breathing

1. Body streamlining.
2. Keeping the legs up.
3. Water level at hairline.
4. Arms remain opposite one another.
5. Head turns to the side for inhalation.
6. Head is face down for exhalation.
7. Complete exhalation.

### Some Common Stroke Defects

1. Arms
   a. Hand or hands pull too far across the body on the underwater pull.
   b. Lifting hands out before they pass the hips.
   c. Making too wide an arm recovery.
   d. Carrying hands too high during recovery.

2. Legs
   a. Keeping the ankles too stiff.
   b. Kicking too deeply.
   c. Kicking from the knees.
3. Breathing
   a. Holding the head too high.
   b. Lifting the head to breathe.
   c. Turning the body to breathe.

### Freestyle Stroke Drills

1. Legs
2. Arms and Whole Stroke

# 4. *Backstroke and Double-Arm Backstroke*

The backstroke usually takes one of two forms. When using the term "backstroke," I am referring specifically to the stroke known as the "back crawl." A variation of this is the "double-arm backstroke," which combines the inverted breaststroke kick with the back crawl arm stroke, but with both arms pulling at once. Both types of the backstroke can be used for fitness as well as for competition.

Both, also, have the distinct advantage over the other competitive strokes that stroke mechanics need not be compromised to allow for breathing because the head is constantly in a face-up position. But to those of you who have a natural aversion to being upside down, going blindly into the unknown, I extend my sympathetic understanding. I have often thought that in several ways backstroke is the most peculiar and frightening of all the strokes, although I have managed some degree of success with it. Furthermore, it has neither the flair and challenge of the butterfly nor the speed of freestyle. And, perhaps most important, a backstroker does not have the visibility that the breaststroker, above anyone else, has.

The backstroker must work from a position that, although excellent for breathing, does not allow him to see what is coming, be it the wall, another swimmer, or a lane marker. And I believe that this lack of visibility creates a certain insecurity for some swimmers that is akin to the unwillingness some beginners express when asked to put their faces in the water. The reason they are afraid is that they close their eyes and therefore can't see. But when these beginners put on swim masks so that they could freely open their eyes underwater, the change is amazing. Almost without hesitation, all gladly put their faces in the water.

Why, you might ask youself, should I purposely turn myself upside down in the water and risk battering my head against tile or teammate when I could just as well swim right side up and probably go faster too? There are several answers. If you are a competitor, you might find that for no explainable reason you just happen to beat more of your competition in backstroke than in other events. Or even if you are not a competitor, you might simply find it comfortable. Also, if you are interested in endurance swimming, you might find that the double-arm backstroke is quite relaxing because of its relatively long glide. In my own training, I have found that another advantage of backstroke is that if the water temperature is unappealingly warm as is sometimes the case in pools used extensively for teaching, I feel more comfortable and become less fatigued swimming with my face out of the water.

Whatever your reasons for deciding to swim backstroke, your task becomes one of maneuvering your body while on your back in such a way that your arms and legs can best push in a backward direction against the water. (Remember Newton's Third Law of Motion?) And the more efficiently you do this the less energy you will need to move forward in the water.

As mentioned, I will deal with both the conventional backstroke (back crawl) and double-arm backstroke. I will first present a complete discussion of backstroke, since this is the more popular; then I will go into the variations involved in double-arm backstroke.

## UNDERWATER ARM PULL

As with freestyle, if you can press your hand against water that is not moving, you can push yourself further forward with each stroke than if you press your hand against water that is moving. So, just as when you swim freestyle, you should make an elongated "S" pattern (see Figure 4.1) with your hands in backstroke, although you will probably find that this is slightly more difficult when you are on your back than when you are on your stomach.

Your hand should travel approximately 12 to 18 inches (about 30 to 45 cm.) below the surface, depending upon

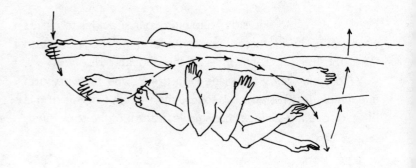

Figure 4.1  **Underwater elongated "S" pull pattern**

your height, before you begin to push toward your feet. Figure 4.1 also clearly shows the hand, palm down, pushing downward toward the bottom of the pool when completing the propulsive phase of the arm stroke at the end of the S pull. Once the thrust from the hand is complete, notice that the hand rotates to a position nearly perpendicular to the surface so that the thumb leaves the water first, thus minimizing resistance. For the same reason, the little finger enters the water first at the beginning of the arm stroke, forming a 90-degree angle with the surface.

Also as in freestyle, elbow bend and body roll play a significant role in making the arm stroke as efficient as possible. Leverage against the water is greatest when you pull with a bent arm. But in order to pull with a properly bent arm, your body must roll to one side, allowing your shoulder to dip as your pulling hand passes your shoulder. (The shoulder lift on the opposite arm contributes to this shoulder dip.)

When your body rolls (see Figure 4.2), the recovery arm encounters less resistance because the shoulder of this arm is lifted above the surface, causing less drag; at the same time, the pulling arm goes deeper, allowing it to push constantly against still water.

## ARM RECOVERY

But in order for you to lift the shoulder of your recovery arm to a maximum height, you must be sure to keep your recovery elbow completely straight and to bring your arm

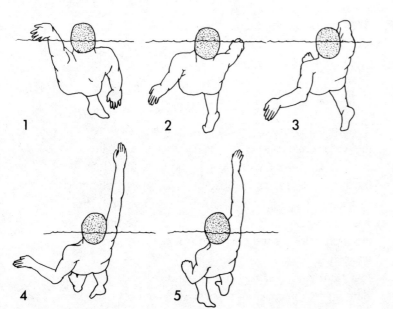

Figure 4.2  **Underwater elbow bend and body roll**

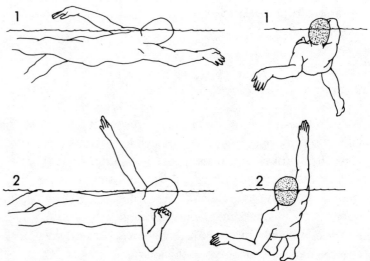

Figure 4.3  **Out-of-water arm recovery**

directly over your shoulder in a line perpendicular to the surface. See Figure 4.3.

Continue this perpendicular line until your hand once again enters the water behind your shoulder. And in case you don't have enough to remember already, don't allow your hand to enter behind your head, since this will tend to make your body move laterally and travel off its designated forward course. As mentioned, your little finger should enter the water first, forming a 90-degree angle with the surface to minimize resistance and so that your hand does not carry air with it into the water, thereby decreasing the effectiveness of your push against the water. See Figure 4.4.

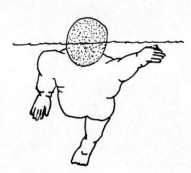

Figure 4.4  **Arm and hand entry**

## KICK

In backstroke, as in freestyle, the key to efficient kicking is ankle flexibility. The more fully you can extend your ankles, the more of your foot you can use to push against the water. But in backstroke, unlike freestyle, the upbeat rather than the downbeat is the power phase of the kick. Therefore, the knees bend slightly on the upbeat, but they should be kept straight on the downbeat, as in Figure 4.5. You must be careful not to let your knees break the surface, or your feet will follow a bicycling motion which is far less efficient than kicking with your knees below the surface.

The distance between your feet when they are farthest apart should be about 12 to 16 inches (about 30 to 40 cm.). For added propulsion, your toes should be turned slightly inward during the upbeat of your kick (see Figure 4.6). This will cause your feet to push backwards more than upwards against the water.

You should use a six-beat kick for every complete arm cycle when swimming the backstroke, for a strong propulsive force from the legs is even more important in backstroke than in freestyle. The reason for this is that because of the position of your arms when you're on your back, your arm stroke cannot be as efficient as your freestyle arm stroke, so

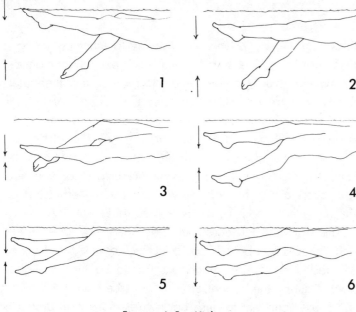

Figure 4.5 **Kick**

downward thrust with your hand at the end of an arm pull, your hips will tend to go slightly to that side, but a strong upbeat from the leg on the opposite side will be your instinctive reaction to avoid such a distortion of body position.

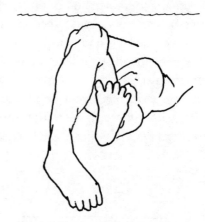

Figure 4.6 **Angle of the toes on the upbeat**

BODY AND HEAD POSITION

The proper body position for backstroke is a compromise between the extremes of carrying the hips very high in the water so as to avoid excessive drag and resistance and carrying the hips low so that the knees and feet do not break

you need a strong push from the legs. Also, because your arms extend a relatively great distance directly above your body during each arm recovery, your legs have the important function of balancing your stroke.

The timing of your leg kicks with the arm stroke will most likely come quite naturally to you. As you give the final

the surface. In other words, the ideal body position is one in which the hips are just below the surface, but the feet and knees at the uppermost point in their motion come to the surface but do not break it, as in Figure 4.7.

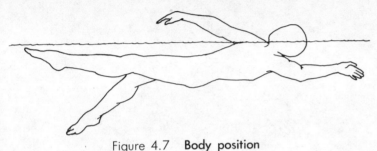

Figure 4.7 **Body position**

In backstroke the body position is, however, primarily determined by head position. See Figure 4.8. When your head is properly situated, your ears are just submerged and the water line is at the middle of your head and just below your chin (Fig. 4.8). To maintain this position, you should keep your eyes open and focus on an object that is approximately 45 degrees from the surface. And you should not allow your eyes to stray from this position or permit your head to move.

If you are afraid of bumping your head against the end of the pool and find yourself moving your head to look for the wall, one solution is to count the number of strokes you take to swim one length, and then count your strokes on each length of backstroke you swim. In competitive swimming meets, a line of colorful triangular flags strung across the pool between poles 5 yards from each end of the pool is used to aid backstrokers in anticipating the wall.

Figure 4.8 **Head position**

In Figures 4.7 and 4.8 as well as 4.3, notice also that at all points in the arm stroke, the arms remain opposite one another.

## BREATHING

Clearly, breathing requires no special body or head motions since your mouth and nose stay clear of the water throughout the entire stroke. But since no natural limitations exist as far as when you should inhale and when you should exhale, it is important that you establish a breathing pattern so that you do not end up inhaling and exhaling incompletely, thereby exhausting yourself needlessly. A good strategy is to start your inhalation when one hand breaks the surface to begin recovery and start your exhalation when the other hand emerges to begin recovery.

## SOME COMMON STROKE DEFECTS

### Arms

1. Using a straight or nearly straight arm for the underwater pull (Fig. 4.9). This greatly reduces the amount of leverage the arm has to push back against the water.

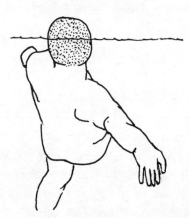

Figure 4.9  **Pulling with a straight arm**

2. Not pulling deeply enough at the beginning of the arm pull (Fig. 4.10). This will mean that the proper S pattern cannot be performed without the fingertips breaking the surface.

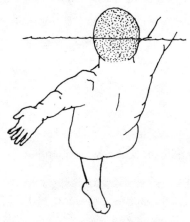

Figure 4.10  **Pulling too shallowly after the hand catch**

3. Not finishing each arm stroke with palms facing down. This causes you to lose the last bit of thrust you could gain from each arm stroke.

4. Hand entering behind the head rather than behind the shoulder. This means that the hand will have to push to the side in order to position itself for the backward push which will cause the upper body to move laterally. Pushing to the

side is also a wasted use of energy.

5. Bending the elbow during recovery (Fig. 4.12). This hinders the shoulder lift of the recovery arm and also causes the hand to cross over behind the head at the beginning of the underwater pull.

6. Hesitating with each arm at the end of the pull (Fig. 4.13). This causes the pulling arm to catch up to the arm that is slow to begin recovery, thereby leaving a "dead spot," where no propulsion takes place in the stroke.

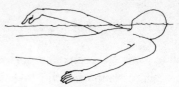

Figure 4.13   **Hesitation with pulling arm**

### Legs

1. Keeping the ankles too stiff (Fig. 4.14). This severely hinders the efficiency of the kick because the feet will mainly move water up and down rather than push backwards against the water.

Figure 4.14   **Stiff ankles**

2. Allowing the hips to ride too low in the water (Fig.

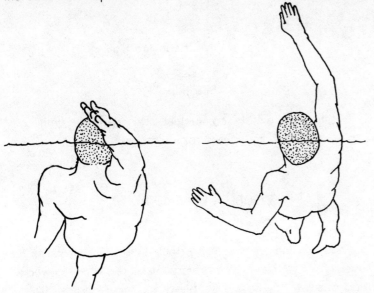

Figure 4.11   **Hand crossing over**

Figure 4.12   **Bent elbow during recovery**

4.15). This causes increased resistance.

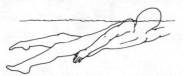

Figure 4.15  **Hips too low**

3.   Allowing the knees to break the surface (Fig. 4.16). This causes a bicycling motion which prevents the feet from pushing backwards against the water as much as they could.

Figure 4.16  **Knees breaking the surface**

4.   Not turning the toes inward. This causes the foot on the upbeat to push water up above the surface rather than backward.

### Head Position

1.   Allowing the head to move. This distorts a body position that permits the least resistance and the greatest visibility.
2.   Holding the head too high (Fig. 4.17). This causes the hips and legs to sit too low in the water, which in turn creates increased resistance.

Figure 4.17  **Head too high**

### Breathing

1.   Failure to exhale completely. This severely limits air intake, and thereby causes rapid fatigue.

## DOUBLE-ARM BACKSTROKE

Many swimmers perfer the double-arm backstroke to the back crawl. When I asked several Masters swimmers whom I had observed doing the double-arm stroke why they liked it better, the most common response was that it was less tiring. This seems logical, because a glide during which the body is completely relaxed comes at the end of each stroke. For this reason, the double-arm backstroke is most often used over longer distances when endurance rather than speed is required, but a few swimmers use it even for sprints.

Another reason for swimming double-arm backstroke was expressed by my teammate Bernice Wayne, who said, "The only way I can get one side of me to do the same thing as the other side when I'm on my back is to have my two sides do the same thing together."

And in double-arm backstroke everything does indeed happen together. Not only do the arms both push then recover at the same time, and the legs both push as well as recover simultaneously, but the arms push when the legs push, and recover when the legs recover. This regularity of motion makes the mechanics of this stroke easy to learn and execute.

## UNDERWATER ARM PULL AND ARM RECOVERY

The technique for performing the underwater arm pull and the arm recovery are the same for double-arm backstroke as for back crawl (see Figure 4.18), with the exception that since body roll is not possible when both arms enter the water simultaneously, the arm pull will be shallower.

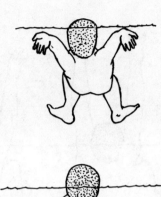
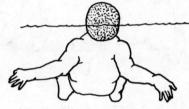
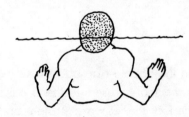

Figure 4.18 **Underwater arm pull**

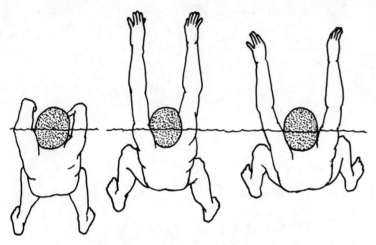

Figure 4.19 **Arm recovery**

## KICK

The kick used in the double-arm backstroke is a "whip" kick which is the same that is used in the breaststroke. At the beginning of the kick the legs are straight and are touching each other. The heels then drop while the thighs remain together, and the toes turn up toward the knees. The feet

then whip out and around in a half circle motion back to the starting position. During the "whip" the knees should not separate more than the width of your shoulders. (See Figure 4.20).

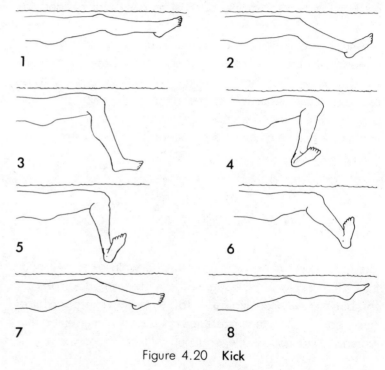

Figure 4.20 **Kick**

The timing of the stroke, as mentioned, is such that your arms push and recover at the same time as your legs push and recover.

## BACKSTROKE STROKE DRILLS

### Legs

1. Sit as close to the edge of the pool as possible, dangling your legs in the water. Kick your legs slowly up and down keeping your ankles as loose as possible. *Purpose*: to gain the feel of the water pressing your toes down during propulsion.
2. Repeat drill 1 above using swim fins. *Purpose*: to exaggerate the feel of the water pressing your toes down during propulsion.
3. Backstroke kick, arms at your sides. *Purpose*: to practice correct body position and to build flexibility in your ankles.
4. Backstroke kick, arms extended behind your head squeezing your ears, and hands held together. *Purpose*: to condition your legs, to streamline your body position, and to practice the proper head position.
5. Backstroke kick, one arm extended behind your shoulder, the other arm at your side with the shoulder raised above the surface. Practice on both sides. *Purpose*: to develop a high shoulder recovery for minimum resistance in the water.
6. Backstroke kick, one arm extended, the other arm at your side with the shoulder raised. Do six kicks on one side, then switch arm positions and do six on the other side. Repeat for the desired distance. *Purpose*: to develop shoulder roll and balance, and to lengthen your stroke.
7. Backstroke kick, one arm extended, the other arm at your side with the shoulder raised. Do three kicks on one side, then switch arm positions and do three kicks on the other side. Repeat for the desired distance. *Purpose*: the same as for drill 6 only the kicking rhythm is like that of the whole stroke.
8. Backstroke kick, one hand either extended behind your shoulder or at your side, the other arm extended straight up at a 90-degree angle to your body. Practice on both sides. *Purpose*: to practice with more resistance, and to work on correct body position.

You may do any of these drills with swim fins to develop feel and to add variety.

## Arms and Whole Stroke

1.   Backstroke with one arm, the other arm at your side with the shoulder raised above the surface when the opposite arm is underwater. Practice on both sides. *Purpose*: to develop shoulder roll.

2.   Backstroke with one arm at a time, the other arm at your side with the shoulder raised above the surface when the opposite arm is underwater. Do three pulls with your right arm, then three pulls with your left, or two pulls with your right, then two pulls with your left. Continue for the desired distance. *Purpose*: to develop shoulder roll and stroking rhythm.

3.   Backstroke with one arm, extend your other arm straight up at a 90-degree angle to your body. Practice on both sides. *Purpose*: to practice stroking with more resistance, while maintaining stroking and kicking power.

4.   Backstroke, stroking with both arms simultaneously. *Purpose*: to develop the proper hand entry position, and to develop the push at end of your stroke.

5.   Backstroke, arms only, stroking with both arms simultaneously. *Purpose*: to force you to complete the push at the end of your stroke.

6.   Backstroke with your arms only, a pull buoy or other flotation device attached to your legs. *Purpose*: to practice your arm pull without distractions, to streamline your body position, and to build arm strength.

7.   Backstroke with your arms only, a pull buoy between your legs, an innertube around your feet. *Purpose*: Same as drill 6, but resistance is increased.

You can do any of these drills with hand paddles to increase resistance and add variety. However, you should exercise caution to see that undue soreness does not develop with the increased strain of more resistance.


## CHAPTER SUMMARY

"Backstroke" refers to back crawl.

"Double-arm backstroke" refers to the stroke that combines the inverted breaststroke kick with the back crawl arm stroke, arms pulling together.

Both types of backstroke have the advantage that no compromise in stroke mechanics need be made to allow for breathing, but have the disadvantage that the swimmer has no visibility in the direction he is swimming.

### Underwater Arm Pull

1.   Elongated "S" pull pattern.

2. Hand goes 12 to 18 inches (about 30 to 45 cm.) deep before beginning the arm pull.

3. Downward thrust at the end of the arm pull.

4. Hand exit nearly perpendicular to the surface, thumb first.

5. Hand entry perpendicular to the surface, little finger first.

6. Body roll, elbow bend, and shoulder dip.

### Arm Recovery

1. Straight arm.
2. Shoulder lift.
3. Hand entry behind the shoulder.

### Kick

1. Ankle extension.
2. Slight knee bend on the upbeat.
3. Straight knee on the downbeat.
4. Depth of kick 12 to 16 inches (about 30 to 40 cm.).
5. Toes turn inward on the upbeat.
6. Six-beat kick.
7. Timing of the kick with the arm stroke.

### Body and Head Position and Breathing

1. Body streamlining.

2. Water line in the middle of the head and just below the chin.

3. Head position so that the line of vision forms a 45-degree angle with the surface, and the ears are in the water.

4. Arms remain opposite one another.

5. Breathing in on one arm, out on the other.

6. Complete exhalation.

### Some Common Stroke Defects

1. Arms
   a. Pulling with a straight arm.
   b. Pulling too shallowly after the hand catch.
   c. Not finishing with palms down.
   d. Hand crossing over on entry.
   e. Bent elbow during recovery.
   f. Hesitating with the arms at the end of the pull.

2. Legs
   a. Stiff ankles.
   b. Hips too low.
   c. Knees breaking the surface.
   d. Not turning the toes inward.

3. Head position and breathing
   a. Allowing the head to move.
   b. Head too high.
   c. Incomplete exhalation.

### Backstroke Stroke Drills

1. Legs.
2. Arms and whole stroke.

# 5. Breaststroke:
# The Oldest and Most
# Stable of Strokes

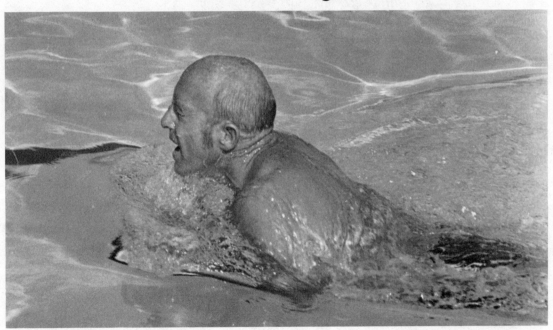

Swimming the breaststroke gives you a rather stable and secure feeling in the water, because neither your arms nor your legs ever come above the surface. This means that your balance in the water does not shift except very slightly when your head rises for inhalation, which is insignificant compared to the shift in balance that occurs in other strokes during the out-of-water arm recovery. But, because your arms do not recover above water in the breaststroke, it is the slowest of the strokes for most people. Visibility, which also contributes to a feeling of security, is excellent, however, and the breaststroke can be quite relaxing over a long distance because of the glide at the end of the stroke.

Unfortunately, a great deal of controversy exists over what the proper mechanics of the breaststroke really are. The reason for this may be related to the fact that more of your body remains underwater for more of the time in breaststroke than in the other strokes, so the problem of greatly increased resistance (since the arms encounter resistance on the recovery as well) is constantly being considered. The timing of the arm stroke with the kick has also become somewhat of a science. So, in my hour of need (would that it were only one hour!) to sort out the many varieties of breaststroke that I have seen and read about, I am grateful to Dr. James Counsilman, whose method seems to make the most sense in regard to the laws of fluid mechanics. The technique I will discuss is very much like Counsilman's, with the exceptions that I advocate placing the hands one on top of the other during the arm recovery and I suggest pushing the hips upward at the end of the kick. But again, you must find the specific method that works best for you, since no one technique is completely correct for every person.

## ARM STROKE

As mentioned, both the arm pull and the arm recovery take place underwater. Your hands move simultaneously through a heart-shaped pattern, your elbows remaining high as your arms bend.

When studying Figures 5.1 and 5.2, don't be misled into thinking that the arm pull and arm recovery are two separate motions. They have simply been drawn as such for clarity. In reality, the arm pull and arm recovery are all one motion; the only hesitation in the stroke comes at the completion of the arm recovery (and the kick) as the arms stretch forward.

In Figure 5.3 notice that the arms extend in front of the shoulders (rather than at the surface) at the beginning and end of each stroke, and that the hands are positioned one on

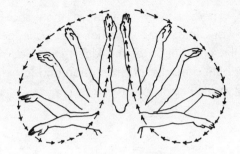

Figure 5.1 **Arm pull**

Figure 5.2 **Arm recovery**

together. As your arms extend forward, the palms turn to face down, one at last resting on top of the other.

top of the other during the arm extension. The palms then turn out as the arms begin pulling to the side. Your arms should bend as the pull continues so that you keep your elbows high and apply maximum backward pressure against the water. When your hands have pulled back as far as your chin, the palms then face one another as they begin to come

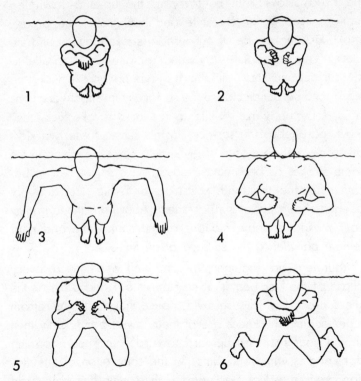

Figure 5.3 **Complete arm stroke**

## KICK

The kick provides a large portion of the propulsive force in the breaststroke. But contrary to the up-and-down leg motions used in the freestyle and backstroke, the breaststroke kick makes use of an out-to-the-side motion, and the feet and legs constantly stay within a plane that is parallel to the surface. In short, in the freestyle-backstroke kick, the legs move perpendicular to the surface (with slight variations caused by body roll) while in the breaststroke kick, they move parallel to the surface. In this sense, these two kicks are completely opposite. They should never be mixed in the same stroke, as beginning breaststrokers sometimes do because they feel that the breaststroke or "whip" kick does not adequately propel or support them. *Above all, the legs must both make the same motions at the same time and must remain parallel to the surface at all times.*

Your legs are together, toes pointed when the recovery phase of the kick begins. (See Figures 5.4 and 5.5.) As the knees drop, feet now relaxed, notice that the thighs remain together until the knees are at their lowest point. Only then should your feet turn upward toward your knees, forming right angles with your shins. At the completion of this motion, your feet kick backward with a whip-like half circle

movement, knees staying not more than shoulder width apart. As your feet come together and your toes begin to point for the completion of the kick, your hips rise slightly — to contribute a last bit of propulsion and to help the arms stretch just a little farther forward.

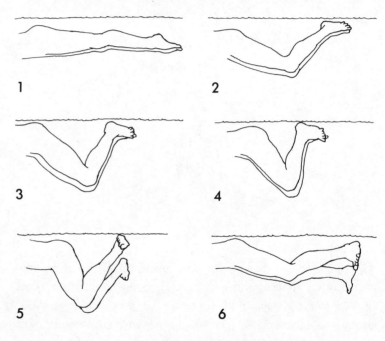

Figure 5.4 **Kick (angle 1)**

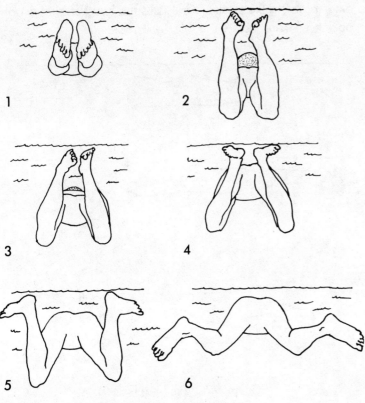

Figure 5.5   **Kick (angle 2)**

Once you feel that you've caught on to the breaststroke kick, listen to your legs as you kick with a kickboard to be sure they are not making any splash. Or if you can, find someone to check your kick for any signs of bubbles or turbulence; this will not be present if your kick is entirely underwater.

## BODY POSITION AND BREATHING

Part of your head must break the surface at all times when you swim breaststroke. But the rest of your body remains completely underwater — near enough to the surface that lifting your head for breathing is easy, and so that your heels are just below the surface during the entire kick. The hips rest in a position just slightly below the heels during all portions of the kick, except when they rise as the feet squeeze together.

As the feet come together and are pointing straight back, and the arms are extended in front of the shoulders, the head is at its lowest and the hips are at their highest. This is precisely the time when you must be careful that your head does not dip below the surface.

During exhalation, the waterline should be at your hairline and during inhalation your chin should just clear the surface. Any excessive up-and-down motion with your head only uses up energy and causes added resistance.

## TIMING

The timing of the arm, leg, and head motions in breaststroke may be a little more difficult than in freestyle or backstroke. But perhaps you will have an easier time mastering the proper timing if you understand that an underwater arm recovery, if your stroke is not timed properly, can cause interruptions in the smooth forward progress of your body through the water. For example, if you were to push back against the water with your arms at the same time as you push back with your legs, then you would be forced to recover your arms at the same time as your legs which means that for approximately half your stroke you would not only have no means of propulsion, but your body would not be streamlined in its recovery position.

This is one clear reason why your arms must begin their pull before your legs begin their kick, as in Figure 5.6. From the starting position, with your arms extended in front of your shoulders and legs pointing straight backwards, you must pull your hands back as far as chin level before your knees begin to drop in preparation for the kick.

Notice, too, that as the hands reach chin level and the knees begin to drop, the shoulders are at their highest point, which makes lifting the head for inhalation easier than at any other place in the stroke. As it rises the head creates an air pocket in front that is suitable for breathing.

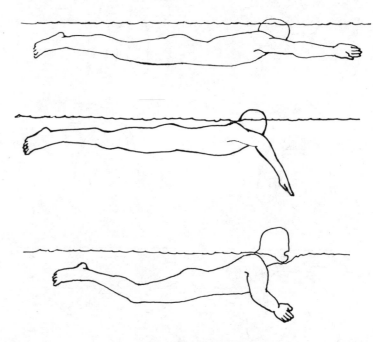

Figure 5.6 **Timing (phase 1)**

As your knees continue to drop, your palms, which have been facing your feet, turn 45 degrees to face one another diagonally and come toward each other.

Once your knees have reached their lowest point, your hands begin to move forward and your palms once again turn 45 degrees to face the bottom of the pool, one palm coming to rest directly on top of the other. See Figure 5.7. As your hands come forward, your face once more submerges for exhalation.

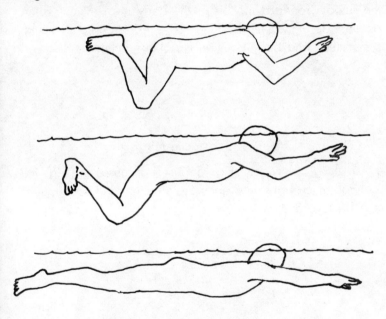

Figure 5.7   **Timing (phase 2)**

Your feet then turn up toward your knees and whip around in a half circle motion as your hands continue to move forward. But just before your feet come completely together, your hips should rise slightly as your arms stretch forward as far as possible.

## STROKE DEFECTS

### Arms:

1.   Arms pulling too widely (Fig. 5.8). This causes the hands and arms to push too much in a sideways direction, and not enough in a backwards direction.

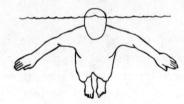

Figure 5.8   **A too wide arm pull**

2.   Dropping the elbows during the pull (Fig. 5.9). This means that only the upper arm, rather than the whole arm, can push back against the water.
3.   Arms hesitating between the pull phase and the recov-

ery phase of the arm stroke. This causes a break in the continuous motion of the stroke and allows the body to sink down in the water, thus creating more resistance. Holding the head up too long during breathing often causes such a hesitation in the stroke.

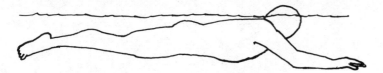

Figure 5.9    **Dropped elbows**

### Legs

1.    Legs not moving parallel to the surface (Fig. 5.10). The rules which govern breaststroke do not permit this.

2.    Toes not turning up toward the knees during the propulsive phase (Fig. 5.11). This causes the feet to slice through the water rather than push back against it.

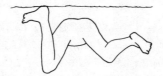

Figure 5.10    **An uneven kick**

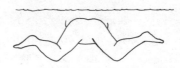

Figure 5.11    **Relaxed ankles**

3.    Kicking too early in the stroke (Fig. 5.12). This destroys the smooth forward motion of the body through the water because during too much of the stroke no propulsion is being generated, and body position is not streamlined.

Figure 5.12    **Kicking too soon**

4.    Kicking too widely (Fig. 5.13). This causes the legs to push too much water in a sideways direction and not enough in a backward direction.

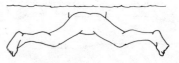

Figure 5.13    **A too-wide kick**

### Head Position

1. Bringing the head up too high during inhalation (Fig. 5.14). This requires extra energy, creates increased resistance, and causes the body to sink down in the water after inhalation.

Figure 5.14  **Breathing too high**

2. Carrying the head too low in the water (Fig. 5.15). The rules that govern breaststroke do not permit the head to go completely below the surface.

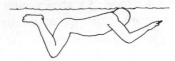

Figure 5.15  **Carrying the head too low**

### BREASTSTROKE STROKE DRILLS

### Legs

1. Breaststroke kick on the pool wall, one hand holding onto the gutter, the other hand flat against the wall two feet below the surface. Do the "whip" kick, making sure that both feet are moving simultaneously and heels are equidistant from the surface. *Purpose:* to develop the proper kicking technique.

2. Breaststroke kick with a kickboard, face in the water. *Purpose:* to practice proper body position.

3. Breaststroke kick with a kickboard, head above water. *Purpose:* to build strength and endurance into your kick.

4. Breaststroke kick, face in the water, arms extended, one hand on top of the other. *Purpose:* to practice proper body position.

5. Breaststroke kick, arms at your sides, hands behind your back. Touch heels to your hands with each kick. *Purpose:* to balance and build power into your kick and to develop the timing for correct breathing.

6. Breaststroke kick next to the wall so the bottom of your foot touches the wall, toes pointing forward, with each kick. Practice on both sides. *Purpose:* to develop the feel of your toes turning up toward your knees, and to even out an unparallel kick if it exists.

7. Breaststroke kick on your back, arms at your sides. *Purpose:* to develop balance, to narrow your kick, and to detect an unparallel kick if present.

8. Vertical breaststroke kick in deep water, hands on top

of your head. *Purpose*: to strengthen your kick.

9.   Alternating "eggbeater" kick (breaststroke kick done one leg at a time), arms in front of you or on your head. *Purpose*: to strengthen your kick.

### Arms and Whole Stroke

1.   Breaststroke pull, lying on your stomach on the pool deck with the gutter or edge of the pool directly below your shoulders, arms extended over the water. Your palms should make contact with the pool wall at the end of each pull. *Purpose*: to learn the proper length of the pull, and to bring your elbows higher.

2.   Breaststroke pull starting with a small wrist scull and progressing to a larger pull. *Purpose*: to develop a feel for the armstroke.

3.   Breaststroke, beginning with a small armstroke, then increasing gradually to a full arm stroke. *Purpose*: to develop coordination and feel for the armstroke.

4.   One-arm breaststroke, other arm extended. Practice on both sides. *Purpose*: to simplify your practice on timing.

5.   One-arm breaststroke, other arm at your side with your hand behind your back. Practice on both sides. *Purpose*: to adjust your position if necessary.

6.   Arms-only breaststroke, a pull buoy or other flotation device attached to your legs. *Purpose*: to strengthen your arms and improve your feel for the pull.

7.   Arms-only breaststroke, a pull buoy between your legs, an innertube around your feet. *Purpose*: to increase strength still further.

You can do any of the above drills with hand paddles to increase resistance and to add variety. You should be careful, however, so that undue soreness does not develop with the increased strain of added resistance.

## CHAPTER SUMMARY

In breaststroke neither your arms nor your legs come above the surface, which makes the stroke both very stable and very slow by comparison to the other strokes. But breaststroke is relaxing and visibility is good.

### Arm Stroke

1.   Simultaneous arm movements.
2.   Heart-shaped arm pull pattern.
3.   One motion for the pull and recovery.
4.   Arm extension in front of the shoulders, one hand on top of the other.

5. Palms face out at the beginning of the pull.
6. High elbows during the pull.
7. Hands pull back to chin level.
8. Palms face down during the recovery, one hand on top of the other.

## Kick

1. Legs must make the same motions at the same time.
2. Legs must stay parallel to the surface.
3. Starting point is with legs in a straight back position, thighs together.
4. Knees drop with thighs still together, feet relaxed.
5. Feet form right angles with shins and whip back in a half circle motion, knees staying close together.
6. Hips rise at the end of the kick.
7. Feet do not break the surface.

## Body Position and Breathing

1. Head breaks the surface at all times.
2. Heels are just below the surface.
3. Hips rest slightly below heels, except at the end of the kick.
4. Waterline is at your hairline during exhalation.
5. Waterline is just below your chin during inhalation.

## Timing

1. Arms begin their pull before the legs begin their kick.
2. When your hands reach chin level, the knees begin to drop.
3. As the knees begin to drop, the head comes up for inhalation.
4. Before the knees are fully dropped, the hands turn and come toward each other.
5. When the knees are lowest, the hands turn and come forward.
6. Face submerges for exhalation as the hands come forward.
7. Feet whip around as the hands come forward.
8. Before the feet come completely together, the hips rise as the arms stretch forward.

## Some Common Stroke Defects

1. Arms
   a. Arms pulling too widely.
   b. Dropping the elbows during the pull.
   c. Arm hesitation between pull and recovery.
2. Legs
   a. Uneven kicking.
   b. Toes not turning up toward the knees.
   c. Kicking too soon.
   d. Kicking too widely.

3. Head Position
   a.  Breathing too high.
   b.  Carrying the head too low.

# 6. *Butterfly and Butterfly With a Breaststroke Kick*

*T*he idea that eventually became the butterfly stroke developed from the breaststroke — probably at the very moment when some coach threw up his or her hands in frustration over the cumbersome nature of an underwater arm recovery and decided to talk a rules committee into accepting an alternative. But this incident, if indeed it happened at all, did not take place very long ago. Butterfly did not become an official stroke in competition until 1952 and it did not become popular until about 1956. So the butterfly has not been in existence long enough to be as refined and perfected as the other strokes.

Also, butterfly is more purely a competitive stroke than any of the others. Because it is generally the most fatiguing stroke, butterfly is not particularly useful over long distances, but rather is useful for short bursts of intensive swimming.

In describing the stroke, I will discuss two types of kick. The first is a dolphin or "fishtail" kick which is the most widely used today. Next, I will explain the mechanics of swimming butterfly with a breaststroke kick, which was the original butterfly stroke and is still used extensively by adults. Keeping the principles in mind which I describe, you must find the method that is best for you since no one technique is completely correct for everyone.

The underwater propulsive portion of the butterfly is much like that of the freestyle, except that the butterfly pull is shallower because shoulder roll is not possible when both arms must pull at the same time. But, as in all of the other strokes, the hands make an elongated "S" pattern so that they always encounter still water.

Notice in Figure 6.1 that the hands push to the sides both at the beginning of the stroke and at the end, and that the hands enter at a 45-degree angle just outside the shoulders (Fig. 6.2).

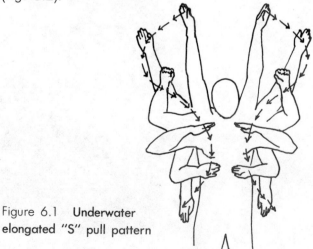

Figure 6.1 **Underwater elongated "S" pull pattern**

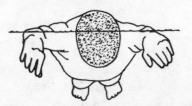

Figure 6.2 **Angle of hand entry**

Also at the entry, your elbows should be slightly higher than your hands to allow a good "catch" on the water after entry (Fig. 6.3). After your hands enter the water, your arms must fully extend as your hands drive down four to six inches for the catch. (See Figure 6.3.)

Figure 6.3 **Elbow position upon hand entry**

Once the catch is made, your hands push a short distance to the side at the beginning of your elliptical pull pattern before pushing diagonally backwards and towards each other, the elbows constantly remaining high, as in the breaststroke. (See Figure 6.4.) Notice in Figure 6.5 that in order for the elbows to remain high while the hands maintain an elliptical pull pattern, the elbows must bend as much as 90 to

100 degrees. When your elbows are at their maximum bend, your hands should, for greatest efficiency, come to within 6 inches of touching one another.

Figure 6.4 **The catch**

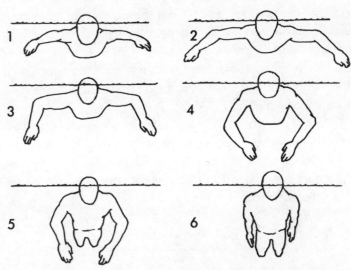

Figure 6.5 **High elbow position throughout pull**

During the final phase of the underwater pull, your hands must make a hard thrust backward and slightly away from your hips; your hands are at a 45-degree angle, with your little finger leading. This helps promote an easy speedy arm recovery.

## ARM RECOVERY

The butterfly arm recovery is not like that of the freestyle, again because body roll is not possible when the arms recover simultaneously. In freestyle the elbows recover high over the water, whereas in butterfly your elbows recover very close to the surface so as to minimize the exertion of lifting both arms at once and to maintain body position as much as possible.

But in both freestyle and butterfly, the wrists remain relaxed throughout recovery, which helps to conserve energy. Notice in Figure 6.6 that the hands barely clear the surface as they swing forward and that the elbows are bent very little, if at all.

Figure 6.6    **Arm position during recovery**

## KICK

The dolphin or "fishtail" kick is used most often in butterfly. This kick is similar to the freestyle flutter kick except that the hips have more freedom to aid in propulsion because the legs move together.

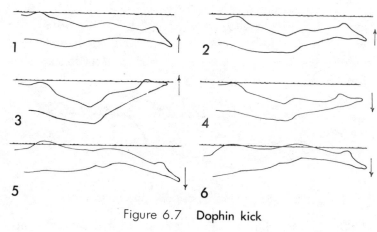

Figure 6.7    **Dophin kick**

As you can see in Figure 6.7, ankle extension is still crucial to an efficient kick, as is bending your knees on the downbeat. But notice how the hips rise and break the surface at the completion of the downbeat, just as the knees reach full extension. The depth of your kick from the point at which your heels break the surface to full knee extension should be 12 to 16 inches.

Most swimmers take two leg kicks for each arm cycle, but a few find that they have a natural tendency to take only one. You should try doing butterfly for awhile with two kicks, then switch to using one only if this comes more naturally to you.

## BODY AND HEAD POSITION

The most efficient butterfly is the one in which your body bends in a loose, natural fashion, much like a flag waving in the wind. At the point of maximum bend in the stroke, the head is lower and the hips are higher than in any other stroke. As you can see in Figure 6.8, the head and shoulders are quite low in the water, but later in the stroke, the head

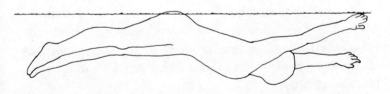

Figure 6.8 **The point of maximum bend**

and shoulders come completely up out of the water (Figure 6.9), which happens in no other stroke.

When your head goes down at the beginning of the stroke, you should concentrate on keeping your ears between your forearms, and when you lift your head to breathe, push your chin slightly forward so that it just clears the surface. If you can master the head position, half the battle is won, because your body will follow the motions of your head.

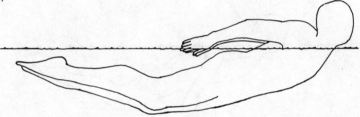

Figure 6.9 **The highest point of the head and shoulders**

## TIMING

In order for your body to bend in a loose natural fashion — the key to an efficient butterfly stroke — proper timing is crucial. Unfortunately, it is not easy. But to make the learning process somewhat easier, I recommend using swim fins because the added propulsion they will afford you will bring your body higher in the water and the arm stroke will be easier to do.

The downbeat of the first kick (or the only kick if you kick just once per arm cycle) should come as your arms enter the water at the beginning of your stroke and your hands stretch forward for the catch. Figure 6.5 shows the position of the arms and head at the beginning of the kick, and Figure 6.8 shows the arm and head position at the end of the kick.

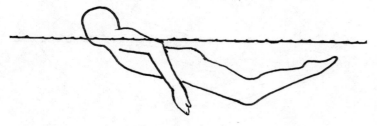

Figure 6.10    **Beginning of the second downbeat**

The downbeat of the second kick (which is missing if you use a single-beat kick) should begin as your hands pass your hips on the underwater pull. (See Figure 6.10.) Kicking at precisely this point should come naturally with practice, and it is useful in three ways. First, it prevents your hands from pulling your hips too low; second, it helps you push your

hands out of the water at the end of your stroke which in turn speeds the recovery; and third, it makes lifting your head to breathe easier.

Notice in Figure 6.11 that during inhalation, the head reaches its highest point when the feet are at their lowest point of the second kick. As soon as inhalation is complete, however, the head should return to a face down position in preparation for the hand entry.

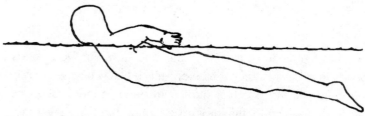

Figure 6.11    **End of the second downbeat**

Rhythm and body bend are optimal when you breathe every other stroke, rather than every stroke. The reason for this is that too many up and down motions will increase fatigue and resistance since so much of your body must rise above the surface to bring your head into the proper position for inhalation.

To simplify my statements about timing, let me close by saying that the first kick should come when your hands are furthest forward, and the second when your hands are furthest backward. The head, then, aided by the second kick, comes up just before your hands emerge from the water at the end of your underwater pull. If you use just one kick per arm cycle, kick when your hands enter the water in the forward position.

## SOME COMMON STROKE DEFECTS

### Arms:

1. Arms enter outside the shoulders (Fig. 6.12). This reduces the leverage to push back, and makes the elliptical pull pattern more difficult.

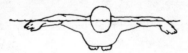

Figure 6.12 **A too-wide arm entry**

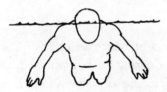

Figure 6.13 **Arms pulling straight back**

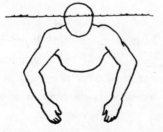

2. Arms pull straight back (Fig. 6.13). This means that you will push against water which is already moving, and thereby reduce the efficiency of your pull.

3. Elbows bend too much on the recovery (Fig. 6.14).

Figure 6.14 **Bent elbow on the recovery**

4. Arm recovery is too high over the surface (Fig. 6.15). This requires too much energy and causes the whole upper body to rise too high during breathing, which in turn increases drag.

Figure 6.15 **A too-high arm recovery**

5. Hand entry is not controlled. If the hands slap the surface when they enter the water, the resistance they encounter in making the catch is increased.

## Legs

1.   Second kick comes just after the first, rather than at the end of the pull. This means that there is no kick at the end of the underwater pull to aid the arms in recovery and to push the hips up.

2.   Kicking from the knees down rather than from the hips (Fig. 6.16). If hip motion does not enter into the kick, body bend and propulsion will be decreased.

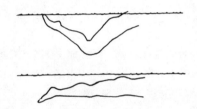

Figure 6.16   **Kicking from the knees only**

## Breathing

1.   Breathing too late in the stroke (Fig. 6.17). This makes recovery and proper hand entry very difficult.

2.   Breathing too early in the stroke (Fig. 6.18). This interrupts the backward push of the hands, which should be continuous.

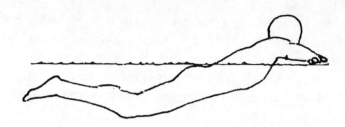

Figure 6.17   **Breathing too late**

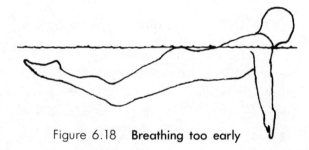

Figure 6.18   **Breathing too early**

## BREASTSTROKE KICK

I have noticed that butterfly with a breaststroke kick is quite popular with adult swimmers, and many people who would not do butterfly at all if forced to use a dolphin kick can manage quite comfortably with a breaststroke kick. I think the reason for this is that, as in double-arm backstroke and breaststroke, a glide at the end of the kick allows a moment of relaxation which delays fatigue. Also, some swimmers obtain more propulsion from a breaststroke kick than from a dolphin kick because of their physiological makeup.

The arm strokes used in the two types of butterfly are identical; only the kicks differ. If you use a breaststroke kick, the kick should come at the same point in the stroke as the first downbeat when a dolphin kick is used — namely, shortly before the arms enter the water in front of the shoulders, as in Figure 6.19.

Body position in the two types of butterfly is the same, except that the breaststroke kick, because it makes use of an out-to-the-side motion rather than a downward motion, does not allow quite as much body bend as the dolphin kick. As for breathing, the movements and the timing are also the same.

Although many of the elements of the two types of butterfly are identical, butterfly with a breaststroke kick does seem to have the advantage that for most swimmers, particularly those who are at least moderately skilled in breaststroke, it is easier to learn and coordinate properly.

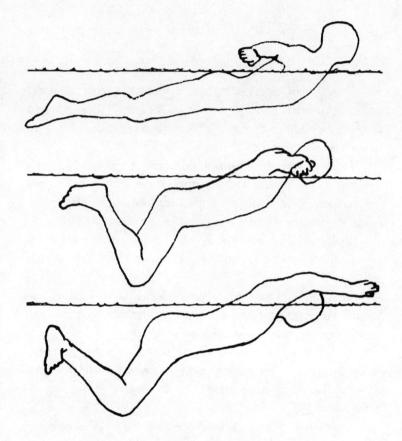

Figure 6.19 **Timing of the arms and legs**

# BUTTERFLY STROKE DRILLS

## Legs

1.  Stand with your feet together, 6 inches from the pool wall, your back toward the wall. "Bounce" your buttocks against the wall to create a dolphin-like action. *Purpose*: to learn the principles of the kick.
2.  Dolphin kick on the pool wall, one hand holding onto the gutter, the other hand flat against the wall 2 feet below the surface. Kick from your hips with loose (not stiff) knees. *Purpose*: to streamline your body in the kicking position.
3.  Dolphin kick, arms extended in front, your face in the water. *Purpose*: to streamline your body in the kicking position.
4.  Dolphin kick, arms at your sides, your face in the water. *Purpose*: to develop a feel for the kick in a position which allows the easiest dolphin action.
5.  Dolphin kick on your back, arms at your sides. *Purpose*: to develop a feel for pushing against the water with the tops of your feet while preventing your shoulders from going up and down.
6.  Dolphin kick underwater, arms extended in front or at your sides. *Purpose*: to improve your feel of the kick.
7.  Dolphin kick, arms extended in front. Do three kicks on the surface, then three kicks underwater. Repeat for the desired distance. *Purpose*: to develop the undulating motion necessary for an efficient kick.
8.  Push off the wall, arms extended, toward the bottom of the pool in shallow water. When your hands touch the bottom, bring your feet down and push off the bottom toward the surface, creating a porpoise-like action. *Purpose*: to develop undulation in your kicking.
9.  Dolphin kick on your side, one arm extended under your head, the other arm at your side. *Purpose*: to improve your feel for the kick.
10. Dolphin kick, your arms extended on a kickboard. *Purpose*: to condition your legs.

You may do any of these drills with swim fins to develop feel and to add variety.

## Arms and Whole Stroke

1.  Six dolphin kicks with your arms extended, then one complete armstroke. Repeat for the desired distance. *Purpose*: to begin working on the coordination of the arms with the legs.
2.  Two dolphin kicks with your arms extended, then one complete armstroke without kicking, stopping your arms in front. Repeat for the desired distance. *Purpose*: to begin

coordinating the arm stroke with the leg kick. (You can learn the timing of the butterfly by doing this exercise, but removing the stop in front with the arms, so that they make a continuous motion.)

3.  Underwater dolphin kick with your arms extended for about 20 feet, come up into the full stroke on the surface. *Purpose*: to establish the kick rhythm to be used with the whole stroke before beginning the arm stroke.

4.  Swim three butterfly strokes on the surface then duck your head and kick three butterfly kicks below the surface. *Purpose*: to develop the dolphin-like action needed for proper body bend.

5.  One arm butterfly swim, your opposite arm extended, breathing to the side. Practice on both sides. *Purpose*: to develop the coordination of the breathing with the arm stroke.

6.  Swim butterfly, taking two strokes with one arm (alternating arms), your other arm extended, then one full stroke with both arms. Repeat for the desired distance. *Purpose*: to develop the proper timing of the kick with the arm stroke.

7.  Butterfly, arms only, a pull buoy or other flotation device attached to your legs. *Purpose*: to develop arm strength and to streamline your body position.

8.  Butterfly, arms only, a pull buoy between your legs and an innertube around your feet. *Purpose*: to develop your arm strength with more resistance.

You can greatly increase the dolphin-like action necessary for an efficient butterfly stroke if you use swim fins during drills. Also, using fins will help you bring your arms out of the water, and help you develop feel and add variety.

## CHAPTER SUMMARY

Butterfly originally developed from the breaststroke, and is a relatively new stroke.

Butterfly is more useful over short distances than for long swims.

### Underwater Arm Pull

1.  Elongated "S" pull pattern.
2.  Hand entry is at a 45-degree angle just outside the shoulders.
3.  High elbows upon hand entry.
4.  Arm extension after the catch is to a depth of 4 to 6 inches.
5.  High elbows throughout the pull.
6.  Elbow bend is 90 to 100 degrees when the hands are closest together.

7. Hard hand thrust backward and away from the hips at the end of the pull.

## Arm Recovery

1. Wrists relax when the hands leave the water.
2. Hands swing forward just above the surface.
3. Elbows are straight or nearly straight.

## Kick

1. Ankle extension.
2. Slight knee bend on downbeat.
3. Full knee extension causes hips to rise and break the surface.
4. Depth of kick is 12 to 16 inches.
5. Heels break the surface on the upbeat.
6. Two-beat versus single-beat kick.

## Body and Head Position

1. Body bend is the key to butterfly.
2. Head and shoulders go both lower and higher than in any other stroke.
3. Ears are between your forearms as your arms extend for the catch.
4. Chin is forward and just clears the surface during inhalation.

## Timing

1. Downbeat of the first kick comes when your arms enter the water in front and begin to stretch forward.
2. Downbeat of the second kick comes as your hands pull past your hips.
3. Head reaches its highest point when your feet are at the bottom of your second kick.
4. Head should come down as soon as possible after inhalation.
5. Breathing every other stroke provides optimal rhythm and body bend.

## Some Common Stroke Defects

1. Arms
   a. Arms enter outside the shoulders.
   b. Arms pull straight back.
   c. Elbows bend too much on the recovery.
   d. Arms recover too high over the surface.
   e. Hand entry is not controlled.
2. Legs
   a. Second kick comes just after the first.
   b. Kicking from the knees down.
3. Breathing
   a. Breathing too late.
   b. Breathing too early.

## Butterfly with Breaststroke Kick

Butterfly with a breaststroke kick is more relaxing and easier to learn for many swimmers.

1. Arm stroke. The arm stroke is the same as for butterfly with a dolphin kick.
2. Kick. A breaststroke kick replaces the first dolphin kick. The second dolphin kick disappears.
3. Body position. Body position is the same, although a breaststroke kick does not permit as much body bend.
4. Breathing. Breathing is the same for both types of butterfly.

# 7. *Getting into Shape*

*O*nce you have accustomed yourself physically and mentally to going to the pool every day and have mastered the stroke techniques at least to the point that you can swim several consecutive lengths using each one (it's okay if you're having trouble with butterfly — everyone does at first), you're now ready to make your training more efficient. The specific training methods presented in the first section of this chapter will serve that purpose. You may also find the training devices described in the second section to be useful in conjunction with these training methods.

## TRAINING METHODS

### Interval Training

Interval training is defined by Dr. James E. Counsilman as that method of training in which regularly repeated periods of exercise at less than maximum intensity alternate with specific periods of rest, sufficiently short so as not to allow full or even nearly full recovery from the preceding span of exercise.[11]

In other words, in order for a physical activity to contribute significantly to your cardiovascular fitness, your heart rate must not drop to a resting state for a period of about one half hour or more, depending upon your level of conditioning. This means that when you exercise, if you stop you must stop only for very short periods of time, or your heart rate will drop rapidly and the benefits of the exercise will be diminished. In fact, numerous experiments performed on training over the years have proved that with a short rest "interval" between consecutive laps of swimming, the effort exerted on each lap can be increased, which in turn will lead to a greater gain in the level of cardiovascular fitness.

You can make the principle of interval training work to your advantage in several ways. One way is to place a rest interval between each swim in a series of swims of equal distance. For example, you can swim 10 × 100 meters, taking exactly 20 seconds' rest between each 100 meters. This is called a *constant rest interval*. Examples of instances when such an interval could be used to advantage are as follows:

☐ During a low-intensity period in a workout which occurs in between periods of high-intensity swimming.

☐ When a large number of swimmers of varying abilities must swim in a very limited space (each swimmer, even the slowest, will get the same amount of rest).

☐ If you are very tired or are having an unusually bad day

then this type of interval can lend some structure to your workout without concerning yourself with how fast you are swimming.

A second type of interval I will call a *constant send-off* interval. Here, you keep the time period between the start of each swim in a series constant; for example, you could swim 10 × 100 meters leaving every 2½ minutes. This kind of interval is appropriate when you want to keep close track of your exact time for each swim in a series. This provides an added incentive to do higher quality swimming with faster heart rates and faster times than with the constant rest interval mentioned above. But due to the intensity of effort often required with the constant send-off type of interval training, it is, however, probably not reasonable to think that you will be able to do more than 40 to 60 percent of your workout using this method of training if you expect to hold times that demand 75 to 85 percent of your maximum heart rate (as you must if you want to see significant improvement).

Both the constant rest and the constant send-off types of interval training will allow you to achieve a higher level of fitness and introduce greater variety into your workouts than will continuous swimming. In addition, both types provide a systematic way to monitor your progress and can easily be adapted to meet individual needs.

To add further variety to your workouts, you can do some variations of these two types of interval training. For example, rather than swimming a constant distance and taking a constant rest interval you could increase the distance until you can no longer hold a constant speed, while keeping the rest interval constant.

Example:
    Swim one length, then rest 10 seconds
    Swim two lengths, then rest 10 seconds
    Swim three lengths, then rest 10 seconds
    Swim four lengths, then rest 10 seconds
    and so forth.

The object is to hold a constant speed and a constant number of strokes per length.

Another suggestion would be to decrease your interval send-off time over a series of swims in order to increase stress:

Example:      10 × 100 meters

              100 meters leaving every 2 minutes — 3 times.
              100 meters leaving every 1:50 — 3 times.
              100 meters leaving every 1:40 — 3 times.

100 meters leaving every 1:30 — 1 time.

The object is to see if you can make each interval (or some other interval that you decide upon beforehand) without going past the designated send-off time.

Many other variations exist and you can certainly try your own hand at making up new ones, keeping Counsilman's definition in mind.

## Repetition Training

Interval training of any kind primarily improves endurance and aerobic capacity (both of which are crucial to cardiovascular fitness). If you also want to improve your speed and your anaerobic capacity, you should use other methods of training in addition to your interval training. One such method is called *repetition training*.

Repetition training works on the same principle as interval training in that fitness and adaptation to physical stress are achieved through exposure to alternate periods of stress and rest. By definition, however, repetition training is done with longer rest intervals than interval training. Repetition training is defined by Dr. James E. Counsilman as that method of training in which regularly repeated periods of exercise at very high intensity alternate with specific periods of rest, long enough to allow virtually full recovery from the pre-ceding span of exercise.[12]

Example:

4 × 100 meters — taking one and one half to two minutes or more of rest between each 100 meters.

As the example shows, the number of swims in a repetition series is generally lower than the number of swims in an interval series, because of the intensity of effort involved and the greater length of time needed for rest during repetition training.

But the longer rest means that repetition swims can be done at very near top speed. In fact, this type of swimming should probably be used mostly on days when the very highest quality swimming is desired, and it should not come immediately after strenuous endurance work, when you are already quite fatigued.

Long rest repetition swimming is usually done by competitive swimmers during practice sessions within a few days of competition, when their total workout distance is low, consisting only of easy, loosening up swimming and high quality swimming as close to race speed as possible. Such a session is called a "taper."

But just as a taper is a culmination of many weeks or months of hard training, so is repetition training "icing on the cake" (perhaps an inappropriate metaphor for athletes) that comes after a main course of short rest training. In other words, it is not likely that you will whip yourself into good physical shape very quickly or very well on a diet high in repetition training. But at the same time, if you never do any repetition training you will not gain the fullest benefit of the other methods of training you have been using. So if you've been working hard, go ahead, rest a little extra, and gain the additional "edge" you deserve.

Ideally, once you are in good enough shape to push yourself beyond 60 percent of the difference between your resting and your maximum heart rate, you should do 40 to 60 percent of your workout using interval training, as well as repetition training in amounts not to exceed 5 to 10 percent of your workout, when high quality is desired. With this approach you will have the best chance of becoming proficient at both long distance and short distance swimming because you will be conditioning your body to swim at a moderate speed for long periods of time (interval training), and for a moderate length of time at a high speed (repetition training).

## Overdistance Training

Overdistance training, as the name indicates, is the practice of swimming longer-than-race distances in order to give the body general conditioning for shorter distances. The principle behind overdistance training, according to Counsilman, is that forcing the body to adapt to long continuous periods of moderately increased heart rate and oxygen demand will lead the swimmer to achieve greater heart stroke volume (more blood pumped per heart beat), a slower resting pulse rate, and improved ability of his lungs to extract oxygen from the air.[13]

Overdistance training can be a very useful method if you have reasonably good stroke mechanics and strength, but you have been away from swimming for some months or years so you are not in condition to do high intensity training. During overdistance training you can readily stay within 60 percent of the difference between your resting and your maximum heart rate, which has already been suggested for swimmers who are new to training or returning to training after a long absence. For competitive swimmers, off-season and early season swimming is usually of the overdistance type because stress is prolonged rather than momentarily intense and therefore is not such a shock to the body.

The length of the swims in overdistance training can range from 200 to 300 yards to 1650 yards or more, depending upon your level of conditioning and your goals. The 1650 yard freestyle is the longest race in Masters competition and if you are preparing for this event your overdistance training should consist of longer swims and should occupy a greater percentage of your workout time than if you plan to specialize in shorter events or another stroke.

## Sprint Training

Sprint training consists of very short fast swims at top speed.

Example:

10 × 25 meters — 10-20 seconds rest between each swim.

10 × 50 meters — 20-30 seconds rest between each swim.

For even greater bursts of speed, you might want to go the width of the pool or from the end of the pool to a rope stretched across the pool 10 to 15 meters down.

Sprint training has one aspect in common with repetition training in that both operate on the principle of stress through intense speed, which in turn means that both build strength and power more than endurance and both increase anaerobic capacity (your body's level of ability to absorb stored oxygen) more than aerobic capacity. But some important differences exist as well, and these should not be overlooked.

First, the length of the rest period during sprint training is shorter than in repetition training. This means two things: (1) during a given period of time in a workout you can swim more yards using sprint training than repetition training, so sprint training is useful in more workout situations when time is limited than is repetition training; and (2) while the intensity of effort expended with both types of training may be similar, the quality of each swim will be just a little higher with repetition training than with sprint training, which means that repetition training (as mentioned) should probably be reserved for instances when effort of the "extra special" type is expected, while sprint training should be more of an everyday occurrence.

Second, the key to sprint training is that a "sprint" by definition is a distance short enough to be covered virtually at top speed, whereas the key to repetition training is that the number of repetitions is sufficiently low so that each swim, regardless of the distance (which in most cases should not exceed 100 meters), can be done at maximum effort.

But precisely because sprint training involves the shortest distances, it plays an important role in the adaptation of the body to stress. Most importantly, sprint training, according to Counsilman, causes the muscles to adapt by improving their ability to contract quickly against force.[14] You must be careful, however, not to overdo your sprinting, particularly in the beginning, because muscle soreness develops quite easily with this type of training, especially if you have not first warmed up with a few laps of easy swimming. Also be sure to follow your sprinting with easy swimming (a swim-down).

So, since sprint training builds power into the muscles while interval training builds endurance, it is important to do sprint training often if you want to be a good all-around swimmer. Depending upon the length of the events in which you would like to specialize, you should spend anywhere from 25 to 50 percent as much time on sprint training as you do on interval training.

To add variety to your sprint training, try the following variation of the example given above. The object is to try to increase your speed as the distance decreases.

Example:

        1 × 75 meters
        Rest 20-30 seconds
4 ×     1 × 50 meters
        Rest 10-20 seconds
        1 × 25 meters

## Speed-Variation Training

Speed-variation training, as the name suggests, is a method that makes use of varying speeds for its effectiveness. For a given distance (usually at least 200 meters), you alternate lengths of fast swimming with lengths of slow swimming.

Example:
    1 length slow.
    1 length fast.
    1 length slow.
    2 lengths fast.
    1 length slow.
    3 lengths fast,
    and so forth.

Speed-variation training is much like interval training of the constant rest type in that intermittent periods of partial recovery (the slow lengths) come between lengths of hard swimming. Recovery, of course, is a bit slower because the body is not at complete rest, but the recovery periods are often a little longer than those used in interval training.

This type of training should be used during low stress periods in your workout or on "low key" days; it is a means to develop endurance rather than speed. Also, when a large group of swimmers of varying abilities are present at a workout, speed-variation can be introduced periodically in the session so that slower swimmers who may get behind and lose their rest time do not end up swimming hard every length with no letup.

### Hypoxic Training

Hypoxic training is a method of training in which you force your body to adapt to oxygen debt by limiting your breathing during exercise. What this means for you, the swimmer, is that rather than breathing with every stroke, you must breathe every other stroke, or every third, or fourth, and so on. Or you can use the following pattern on each length that you swim.

Example:
1 stroke without a breath.
1 stroke with a breath.
2 strokes without a breath.
1 stroke with a breath.
3 strokes without a breath.
1 stroke with a breath.
4 strokes without a breath.
1 stroke with a breath,
and so forth.

The most important physiological change that occurs as a result from hypoxic training is that the number of mitochondria in the muscle fibers increases. Mitochondria are important to an athlete's performance because they are the small cellules (about 100 to 1000 per muscle fiber) that release "fuel" into the muscles in the form of oxidized foodstuffs.[15] And because every swimmer needs muscle fuel, hypoxic training can benefit the distance swimmer as much as the sprinter, the fitness swimmer as much as the serious competitor. In short, according to Counsilman, hypoxic training is a valuable training technique because it both increases the efficiency of your muscles at the cellular level, and enhances your ability to tolerate the pain of oxygen debt.[16] (Oxygen debt occurs when the body uses up more oxygen that it takes in.)

Still, with the idea of general conditioning in mind, if we look at the effects of hypoxic training on heart rate, we can see yet another value of this method of training. During hypoxic swimming, it is' possible to boost your heart rate higher than if you swim the same distance under similar stress but with a normal breathing pattern. A study was conducted at Indiana University on college swimmers to determine what effect various breathing patterns would have on heart rate immediately following the last swim in a series. Table 7.1 gives a sample of the data recorded in that study. As indicated, the swimmers, when swimming a standard number of swims in a series (10 × 100 yards or 5 × 200 yards) and keeping the speed and the rest interval the same for each series, recorded higher heart rates when they breathed less often.

Table 7.1   Pulse Rate After Last Effort[17]

| Distance | Breathing every arm cycle | Breathing every 2nd arm cycle | Breathing every 3rd arm cycle |
|---|---|---|---|
| 10×100 yards | 161 bpm* | 164 bpm | 175 bpm |
| 5×200 yards | 150 bpm | 153 bpm | 167 bpm |

*beats per minute

In my own training, however, I have discovered that although I can achieve high heart rates quite rapidly when adding hypoxic breathing to my interval training, I recover to a moderate heart rate more rapidly than I do when I have done a hard series breathing every arm cycle. The reason for this I can only attribute to the fact that I cannot achieve as great a speed when I must limit my intake of oxygen.

According to Counsilman's guidelines below, speed during hypoxic training should be controlled, a statement in response to which I, for no want of breath at the moment, would like to heave a sigh of relief. His recommendation, however, stems not so much, I'm sure, from a sense of sympathy for athletes, as from his knowing that oxygen demand intensifies with speed and that severe deprivation of oxygen can be harmful.

To further understand the concept of hypoxic training, let us look at some of Counsilman's guidelines concerning this method of training.

Guidelines For Use of Hypoxic Training

1.   Holding the breath too long can cause unconsciousness which is a great danger in swimming because the swimmer will sink away from his air supply.
2.   If headaches develop they should disappear within a half hour. If they do not, hypoxic training should be decreased or discontinued and only slowly reinstated.
3.   Hypoxic training should be done at controlled speeds.
4.   The shorter the distance of the swim, the more strokes a swimmer should take between breaths. For example, when swimming 10 × 50 meters, you might breathe every third or fourth arm cycle; but when swimming 4 × 500 meters, you might breathe every second or third arm cycle.
5.   Breathing patterns:
Freestyle and backstroke — breathe every fourth or fifth arm cycle on 25, 50, and 75 meter swims. Breathe every second

or third arm cycle on 100 and 200 meter swims.
Breaststroke — breathe every second or third arm cycle, never forgetting to lift your head as if to breathe so as not to disturb stroke mechanics.
(For butterfly Counsilman recommends a similar pattern as for freestyle and backstroke, but I would suggest that adult swimmers stick to breathing every second arm cycle.)
6. Do not change stroke mechanics when breathing hypoxically. Some swimmers tend to turn the head too long during inhalation or shorten the arm pull in order to take more strokes between breaths.[18]

In addition, you should understand that hypoxic training, perhaps even more than the other methods of training, is a long-range project, for it must be used with caution and avoided when high quality and speed are of the essence. Also, according to Don Schwartz, former coach of the Marin Aquatic Club, the physiological changes brought about by hypoxic training have a six- to seven-day lag time.[19] This means that any hypoxic training you do within one week of a high-performance swim will not help you for that particular swim. Under everyday circumstances, however, I would recommend doing hypoxic training only two or maybe three times a week for one quarter to one third of your interval training time at the most. I think you will probably also find that freestyle seems to be the most compatible stroke to use during hypoxic training.

## Training in Open Water

Training in open water, of course, is not in itself a training method, but some of the elements of pool training can be useful to you if you are an open water swimmer. At the same time, however, the aspects of open water swimming that differ from pool swimming can give you enjoyment either in themselves or as a change of pace.

Obviously, the biggest difference between swimming in open water and swimming in a pool is that in open water it is difficult to figure exact distances. Sometimes there are no markers, and even when markers do exist, currents may affect your course or progress as you swim from one point to another. For this reason, if you plan to do any extensive training away from the containment of a pool, one way to keep track of distance is to swim a measurable distance in still water at least once so that you can count the number of strokes it takes you to swim 200 yards, or a quarter mile, or whatever seems appropriate. This way you can at least estimate (if there is little or no current) how far you are swimming when you have no markers. Another way to measure distance when you swim is to establish approximately how far you swim in a given time and then wear a wristwatch with a second hand to keep time when swimming.

In addition, both counting strokes and keeping track of time are useful in adjusting interval training, repetition training, and speed variation to open water swimming. For example, if you know that normally you take twenty complete arm cycles to swim 50 meters, you could simulate 50 meter swims by sprinting twenty strokes at a stretch and then resting either in a floating position on your back or by swimming easily for a period. Similarly, you can simulate your effort for 50 meter swims by sprinting for the length of time it takes you to swim 50 meters in a pool, then resting, and then sprinting again.

A time piece is also very useful if you want to stop during your open water swim to float for a moment and take your pulse. Once you have done so, you can quickly figure how hard you are working if you know your maximum heart rate.

But perhaps differences between pool swimming and open water swimming other than distance will be as important to you once you have tried both. For example, you may find when you swim in open water that you must swim with your head held quite high and that you must take some strokes with your head completely out of the water so that you can watch landmarks in an attempt to swim in a straight line. Also, if you swim in rough water, you might find it advantageous to learn to breathe on either side when doing freestyle so that you can always breathe away from the waves.

Most importantly, though, you should be sure to take a few simple precautions before entering open water for there can be dangers that are not present in pools. First, check the temperature of the water to see that you can handle it safely for the length of time you intend to swim. Second, check the depth of the water and the type of bottom if the water is shallow. Sharp rocks, coral, or weeds growing on the bottom can cause obvious problems. Third, check carefully for a current and avoid swimming when it is strong. If it is mild, set your course so that you do not swim directly into it and so that you travel with the current at the end of your swim when you are the most fatigued. Common sense applies as well, of course, and will tell you by all means not to overestimate your ability, and not to swim unobserved, no matter how good a swimmer you are.

But as long as you are careful open water swimming is certainly to be enjoyed. Actually, in my opinion, nothing compares with the freedom and exhilaration of an ocean swim when fingers of sunlight filter up toward you from the depths, or when brightly colored tropical fish dart by below you. Or imagine yourself churning away in a forest-encircled lake far from the hustle and bustle of civilization. These are experiences you won't find in a pool.

## TRAINING DEVICES

### Pace Clock

A pace clock is probably the most useful piece of training equipment available next to your swimming suit, cap and goggles. It has a large face, 36 inches (about 1 meter) in diameter with two hands — a second hand and a minute hand. The numbers on the face are 3 inches (about 8 centimeters) high for easy visibility from as far away as 25 meters (Fig. 7.2). Such a clock can be mounted on the wall or stood on the pool deck; it is extremely useful in checking heart rate and in doing interval training, repeat training, overdistance

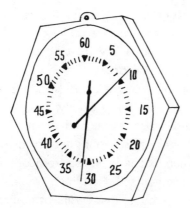

Figure 7.2 **Pace clock**

training, and sprint training. Also, if swimmers can see on the clock when they are to begin each swim, this frees the coach to watch the swimmers' strokes rather than watching the clock.

Any number of workout variations can be produced when all swimmers have a common time reference around which to do their various exercises in the water. For example, to break the routine of doing regular interval sets, such as 5 × 100 meters or 10 × 50 meters leaving at specific times, you could challenge yourself by allowing ten minutes on the clock to do as many 25-meter or one-lap swims as you can, taking ten seconds of rest between each swim. (This kind of exercise works best if the distances are short, because you must otherwise improve a great deal before you will be able to increase the number of swims you are able to complete in the given time period). Also, you can do a set of one lap swims using each of the four strokes and see how fast you are in a given stroke as compared with the others.

Another variation is to give yourself a certain period of time such as five minutes or ten minutes, and see how far you can swim in that length of time, checking the clock at some of the turns. If you do such a swim periodically, you will be able to note your improvement. This is an excellent exercise to use when kicking only, because you have your head out and have full view of the clock.

When a group of swimmers is doing broken swims (swims with short rest periods interjected at given points) a pace clock is indispensable, since swimmers will all come into the wall at different times and therefore must measure their own rest interval. A personal timekeeper for each swimmer, though it would be ideal, is usually not feasible.

When you are learning to swim multilap swims such as 100 meters, 200 meters, or 500 meters, at an even pace, a pace clock can be invaluable if you check the clock at each turn, or every second or fourth turn, to see that you hold your lap times even. Or you can try doing "negative split" swims in which your lap times drop or "descend" with each lap; this is an excellent way to improve your resistance to fatigue.

### Kickboard

A kickboard is a nearly rectangular piece of buoyant material such as styrofoam, about 30 inches (75 cm.) long and about 15 inches (44 cm.) wide. Kickboards serve as an aid in (1) learning the proper mechanics of kicking; (2) building leg strength necessary for efficient swimming; and (3) providing variety in daily workout sequences.

When you use a kickboard to learn the proper mechanics of kicking, the legs can be isolated from the rest of the stroke so that you can concentrate solely on kicking motions while maintaining body position. You should precede kickboard work with kicking drills done in a horizontal position while holding onto the side of the pool with your hands.

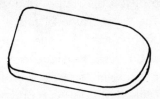

Figure 7.3   **Kickboard**

A kickboard is also invaluable in building leg strength because you can put all the stress of moving the body forward on the legs. This can rapidly bring on a high heart rate because the heart must pump a tremendous volume of blood to the large muscles that are farthest from it. Leg strength contributes to the power needed for fast sprints, and it is crucial to a hard finish at the end of a race or a long swim, for a strong kick is needed to maintain good body position. Leg strength is also necessary for a good push off the wall and an effective dive.

A kickboard can also be used simply to provide a welcome change of pace in your workout. And if you make swimming a regular part of each day, you will want to introduce variety into your training sessions to keep up your interest.

### Swim Fins

Swim fins are made of flexible rubber and should fit snugly around your feet. The "shoe" type of fins, which cover the whole foot except for the toes, is better than the type with the adjustable strap because the shoes stay on better and are more comfortable. Blisters can develop if fins are worn for long periods of time, but if this is a problem, wearing a thin pair of socks under the fins will help.

Swim fins are another training device you can use to add some variety to your workouts and also to help you develop a "feel" for the water with your feet. They are particularly good as an aid to learning the stroke technique used in butterfly, because the extra power and undulating motion provided by the fins allow a swimmer to get his arms out of the water at the end of each stroke. This assistance brings the swimmer a step closer to performing the butterfly with the flowing, uninterrupted arm motion that is characteristic of skilled performers of this stroke.

When used in backstroke, fins can be quite helpful in establishing and maintaining body position. A common error when kicking and swimming backstroke is that the feet are too low in the water and therefore cause unnecessary drag. With the added propulsion that fins can create, the proper position is easier to maintain, particularly when fatigue sets in.

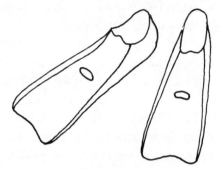

Figure 7.4  **Swim Fins**

The important aspect of fins is that they make acquiring good stroke habits in butterfly and backstroke easy and bad ones difficult. And I believe that once the good habits are formed with fins, a swimmer will have a better chance to keep those good habits without fins.

### Pull Buoy

A pull buoy is a flotation device made from two solid cylinders of styrofoam or other buoyant material fastened together with a strap (Fig. 7.5). It is held between the legs with one cylinder in front of the thighs and one behind them. This isolates the arms so that more concentrated work can be done on the arm stroke.

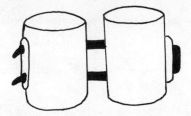

Figure 7.5 **Pull buoy**

Arm pulling generally does not bring about as high heart rates as does swimming or kicking, because the blood does not have to travel to the legs — the farthest area of the body from the heart. Pulling, therefore, is an excellent exercise to do between hard series of swimming or kicking when partial but not complete recovery from stress is desired. This is also a good time to use the hand paddles or other resistance devices. And, as with other aids, you can add variety to your workouts by doing pulling drills.

### Hand Paddles

Hand paddles are simply plates of plastic which fit on each of your palms and attach with rubber tubing to your fingers or hands, depending upon which model you choose. Each paddle should be ½ to 1 inch (1.4-2.5 cm.) larger than your palms on each side. Some hand paddles have a "lip" extending away from the wrist so that if you attempt to lift your hand from the water before reaching the end of your stroke, you will encounter significant resistance, which will in turn encourage you to finish your stroke.

Hand paddles are excellent for strengthening shoulder, chest, and back muscles because of the increased resistance of pushing a larger "hand" through the water.

If paddles are used during pulling, heart rate will increase, because of the added resistance, and they will add stress to a pulling series. You should ease into your use of paddles and take care not to overdo it, since too much work can cause soreness and muscle strain.

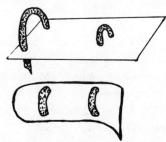

Figure 7.6 **Two types of hand paddles**

## Resistance Devices

Resistance devices of all types are made ranging from vests with cup-like pockets to catch water, to swimming suits worn two or three on top of each other. With the use of "skin suits" in the United States in 1974, a type of near hysteria arose over the whole concept of drag. The belief was (and seemingly still is) that if competition suits made of lycra fit like a second skin, then swimming attire with extra drag would be desirable for practice sessions to offset the stream-lined effect of skin suits for competition. Other resistance devices include small innertubes, each twisted in a figure 8 around the ankles during pulling drills, kickboards with scooped bottoms, and extra articles of clothing, such as T-shirts, sweatshirts, or shorts worn during training.

## CHAPTER SUMMARY

**Interval Training**—submaximal periods of exercise alternating with controlled rest periods.
1. Constant Rest Interval — interval of rest remains constant regardless of swimming time.
2. Constant Send-Off — interval between the start of each swim remains constant regardless of rest time.

**Repetition Training** — maximal periods of exercise at near top speed alternating with long rest periods.

**Overdistance Training** — training at distances greater than the distances for which you specialize.

**Sprint Training** — short, fast, all-out swims done with moderate rest.

**Speed Variation Training** — training in which some lengths of a swim are slow and some are fast.

**Hypoxic Training** — training in which you limit breathing while exercising.

**Training in Open Water**

### Training Devices

**Pace clock**
**Kickboard**
**Swim fins**
**Pull buoy**
**Hand paddles**
**Resistance devices**

Workouts:

| | |
|---|---|
| 400 meters | warmup |

1 × 400 meters kick doing 100 yards of each stroke (over-distance kick training)

4 × 100 meters freestyle, leaving every 2 minutes (interval training—constant send-off)

8 × 50 meters freestyle, paddles and innertube, breathing every 4th stroke, leaving every 1:15 (hypoxic pull, resistance device training)

16 × 25 meters 4 of each stroke, leaving every 45 seconds (sprint training)

| | |
|---|---|
| 200 meters | swim-down |
| 2,200 meters | total |

| | |
|---|---|
| 300 meters | warmup |
| 600 meters | freestyle, breathing every second stroke (overdistance training) |

6 × 100 meters breaststroke, with 20 seconds' rest between each (interval training—constant rest)

4 × 75 meters butterfly with fins, 15 seconds' rest (interval training—constant rest, fins)

4 × 75 meters backstroke with fins, 15 seconds' rest (interval training—constant rest, fins)

| | |
|---|---|
| 200 meters | swim-down |
| 2,300 meters | total |

| | |
|---|---|
| 200 meters | warmup |
| 200 meters | 1 length easy, 1 length hard (speed-variation training) |

4 × 125 meters doing 2 lengths of your weakest stroke and 1 length of the three others, leaving every 2:30 (interval training—constant send-off)

| | |
|---|---|
| 200 meters | freestyle pull with pull buoy and paddles (training device drill) |

5 × 100 meters freestyle breathing every 2nd stroke on length 1, every 3rd on length 2, and every 4th on lengths 3 and 4, leaving every 2 minutes (hypoxic training)

4 × 50 meters stroke of your choice from a dive, leaving every 2 minutes (repetition training)

| | |
|---|---|
| 200 meters | swim-down |
| 2,000 meters | total |

Any of these workouts may be adjusted to suit individual skill levels.

# 8. Starts and Turns

**W**hether or not you are a competitive swimmer, I think that you will find the principles which apply to efficient starts and turns interesting and worth trying.

## STARTS

Starts are basically of two types: out-of-the water starts and in-the-water starts. Out-of-the-water starts are used for freestyle, breaststroke, and butterfly, while an in-the-water start is used for backstroke. The object when doing any type of start is to get off the wall or starting block quickly and to enter the water, arms first, in as streamlined a position as possible. In competition, all starts have two phases, which are called by the starter — "take your marks" and the pistol shot.

### Out-of-the-Water

The out-of-the-water start can be broken down still further into the "grab start" and the "arm-swing start." The grab start is the most recently developed start and is generally considered to be the fastest. The name comes from the fact that when doing this type of start, you grab the edge of the

pool or starting block before you take off. The arm-swing start is used mainly for relay races, because with this type of start, although you get farther out over the water, your feet remain on the edge longer, and only in a relay can you anticipate the exact moment when your feet should leave well enough to swing your arms ahead of time.

You begin the grab start by placing your feet about shoulder width apart, toes over the edge of the pool or starting block (I like to stand slightly pigeon-toed to get more toes over the edge) and standing relaxed, with your hands at your sides. To take your mark, you bend over and grab the edge of the pool or the bottom of the starting block so that your knees are slightly bent and your body weight is as far forward as possible, still allowing you to hold steady. As you hold this position, you should be looking down into the water below your feet. To take off, first pull up against the bottom edge of the surface you are standing on as you lean forward, then swing your arms up, letting your head follow as you make an explosive thrust forward with your legs and ankles. When your body is completely extended over the water, your head should drop slightly so that your arms and upper body enter the water first. (See Figure 8.1.)

The arm swing start (Figure 8.2) is similar, but rather than beginning by grabbing the edge, you begin by letting your

Figure 8.1 **The grab start**

start, you can get a fast take-off by beginning your arm swing when the hands of the swimmer coming in are directly under your hands. Then your feet will be leaving the edge just as the previous swimmer touches the wall.

The entry is the same for the grab start and the arm swing start and it should be studied carefully. It is very important not only that your arms and upper body enter the water

arms hang relaxed below your shoulders as you prepare to dive. Your arms then swing up and backwards. Once your arms come forward, the arm-swing start is the same as the grab start.

Also, in allowing your arms to **hang** when you do a relay

Figure 8.2 **The arm-swing start**

first, but also that your whole body slip into the water as if through a hole. In other words, an efficient start is one in which your body comes into contact with as small an area of the water as possible, while still allowing you a sufficiently shallow entry to surface easily. This will permit you the best combination of distance and speed. Note the entry position in Figure 8.1. (A good way to learn a proper entry is to do a few starts beginning one step back from the edge of the pool or starting block.)

### In-the Water

When doing an in-the-water start such as you use for backstroke, diving through a "hole" is also important, but since you are already in the water when you begin, the object is to bring your body up over the water as you thrust backward away from the pool wall.

Notice in Figure 8.3 that you begin by grasping the backstroke start rail (if a starting block is available); if not, use the gutter or edge of the pool. Then bring your knees up into a tuck position, placing your feet against the wall, either next to each other or one slightly higher than the other.

To take your mark, pull your body up nearly out of the water by bending your elbows. To take off, throw your arms around to the sides until they are directly behind your head,

arching your back and lifting your chin as your arms come around. But be careful not to throw your arms up over your body rather than to the sides, for this will hinder your backward motion and make your entry too deep.

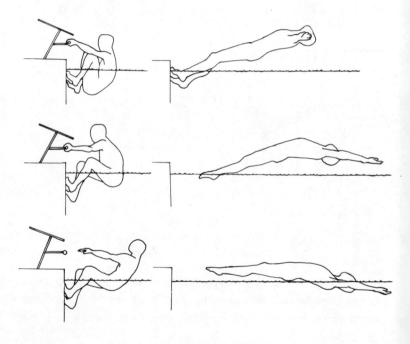

Figure 8.3   **The backstroke start**

## TURNS

Turns, too, are of two types: "flip turns" and "open turns." You can use an open turn (open referring to the fact that the body is not in a tight tuck position) with any of the strokes, but in freestyle and backstroke you have the option of using a flip or somersault-like turn, which, if done properly, is usually faster than an open turn.

### Freestyle Flip Turn

The freestyle flip turn closely resembles a front somersault, as you can see in Figure 8.4. Because the chin is lowered as either one or both arms drive backward toward the hips, a spinning motion is created which brings the legs over the body. Notice, however, that the body begins to come out of the tuck position already before the feet contact the wall. At the same time, the body begins to twist around so that once the feet push against the wall, the side of the body rather than the stomach faces the surface. At this point the body stretches as far as possible off the wall.

An easy way to learn a freestyle flip turn is to take the learning process one step at a time, making use of waist- or chest-deep water. Begin by standing and bringing your upper body down into a tuck position; then, using your arms to push yourself around, do a somersault and return to a standing position facing the same direction as when you began. (You will have to keep your eyes open to do this.) The next step is to go into your somersault from a swimming position, still standing up at completion, facing the same direction as you were swimming. Then try swimming up to the wall and somersaulting but instead of standing up, place your feet on the wall and push off, stomach up. Now you have the complete turn, with the exception of the twist onto your stomach.

Another way to learn a freestyle flip turn is to try a "pike" jump (legs straight, body bending at the waist) towards the wall from 3 to 4 feet away. To do this, first stand on the bottom, then jump forward into a straight-legged somersault, letting your feet stop at the wall and push off on your back. Here again, all you need to add in the end to simulate the complete flipping motion of a flip turn is the twist onto your stomach.

### Freestyle Open Turn

If you prefer to do a freestyle open turn, refer to Figure 8.8 which illustrates the butterfly turn. This turn is like the freestyle open turn in all ways except that in butterfly you touch the wall with both hands, whereas in freestyle you touch with

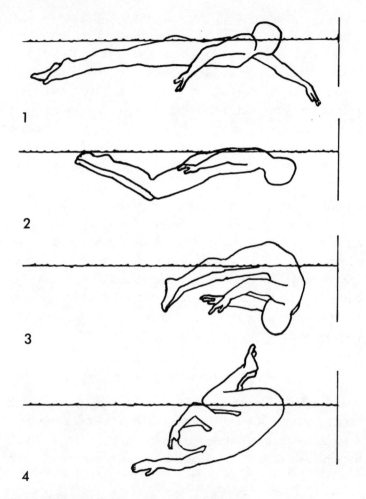

**1**

**2**

**3**

**4**

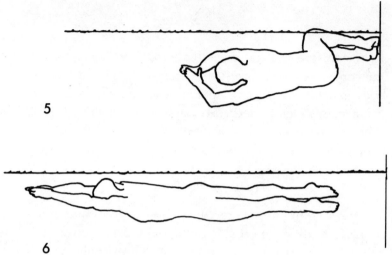

**5**

**6**

Figure 8.4 **The freestyle flip turn**

just one. When doing any kind of open turn, it is important for the sake of conserving energy that you do not pull your body further up out of the water than is necessary to get a breath of air.

### Backstroke Flip Turn

The backstroke flip turn is in several ways simpler and easier to learn than the freestyle flip turn. First, the backstroke turn is really more of a "spin" turn than a flip turn, because you remain on your back throughout, while your head and hips spin around to exchange places. And since your back remains parallel to the surface, it is less likely that you will become disoriented than during the somersaulting action of the freestyle turn. But perhaps the greatest learning advantage of the backstroke turn is that it can be performed entirely (including the push-off) on dry land.

Notice in Figure 8.5 that when the hand comes into contact with the wall the elbow is nearly straight and the fingers are pointing toward the bottom of the pool. Then the knees come up into a tuck position and travel over the shoulder of the contact arm to the same point on the wall where the hand was previously placed. Once the feet are secure on the wall and both arms are extended behind the head, the

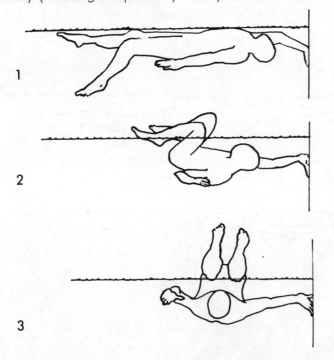

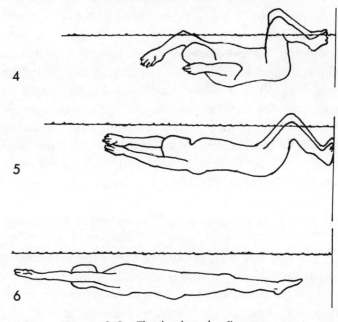

Figure 8.5 **The backstroke flip turn**

push-off and stretch away from the wall takes place.

The key to a successful backstroke flip turn is to keep your eyes open throughout the turn, to keep your upper body constantly parallel to the surface, and to keep your contact hand on the wall for leverage as long as possible before your feet reach the wall.

One way to greatly aid the learning process is to practice this turn on land. Find a slippery floor, such as one made of linoleum, and a scatter rug which if turned nap down should slide easily. Remove your shoes and lay down on the floor with the rug under your back. Extend your arm behind your head, keeping your elbow nearly straight, and adjust your position on the floor so that you can place your palm with fingers pointing down, against the wall. From this position you will be able to perform all of the necessary motions. If you do not have a slippery floor and ample space at your disposal, you can to a limited extent achieve the same results by laying your towel down in a dry corner of the pool deck and practicing bringing your legs around without pushing off.

If you prefer to do a backstroke open turn, the procedure is quite similar except that you should grab the gutter or edge of the pool with your contact hand, and your legs, although in a tuck position, should remain beneath your hips when coming around. Here again, as in all the strokes, be careful not to bring your upper body out of the water at the turn any more than is necessary to get a breath.

## Breaststroke Turn

In breaststroke, unlike in freestyle and backstroke, the open turn is the only choice since a flip turn is not practical when both hands touch the wall at the same time. The breaststroke turn is similar to the freestyle open turn and the butterfly turn. (See Figure 8.6.)

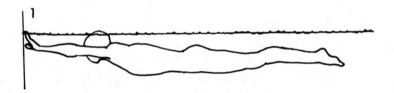

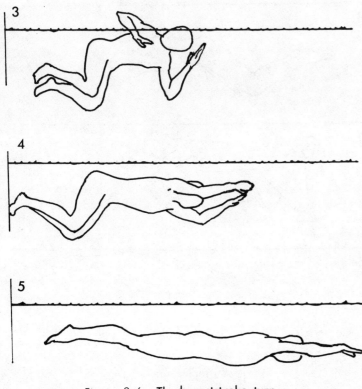

Figure 8.6 **The breaststroke turn**

In Figure 8.6 you can see the stretch with the whole body toward the wall (but the head does not dip below the sur-

face). Both hands touch the wall simultaneously, using, in this case, a "flat wall" touch, meaning that the hands do not grab the gutter or edge of the pool, but simply touch flat. Many coaches say that this is the fastest method of making hand contact with the wall during an open turn, but leverage is a bit more difficult than when you grab the gutter, so work on both and see which best meets your needs.

Notice, too, that both hands are drawn back from the wall (although one at a time) before the feet are placed against it for the push-off, since momentum will carry them in. And observe that the head is slightly lower than the hips and feet on the push-off.

A push-off and stretch off the wall with your head slightly lower than your feet is useful in breaststroke, particularly when you are racing. The rules that govern competition state that the breaststroker is allowed one underwater pull and one underwater kick after each turn and after the start. And since this will contribute to your speed (thus the ruling that your head must break the surface on all but the first stroke off the wall), you would be wise to take advantage of this allowance. You must be careful, however, that your hands do not break apart to begin the second arm pull before your head comes above the surface.

Although the underwater kick is the same that you use in

the breaststroke, the underwater pull differs in that your arms push all the way back to your thighs rather than stopping at shoulder level (Fig. 8.7). As mentioned, an underwater pull and kick follow the breaststroke start as well, which means that you will want to dive just a little deeper when you begin a breaststroke race than any other event.

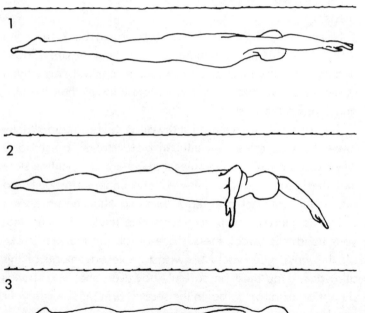

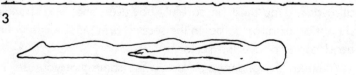

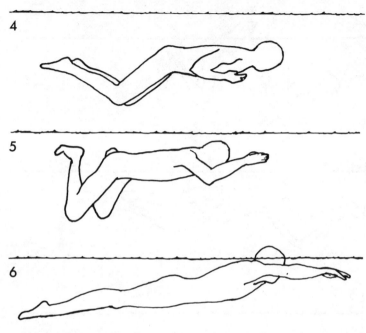

Figure 8.7 **The breaststroke underwater pull and kick**

### Butterfly Turn

The final turn for discussion is the butterfly turn, also an open turn, which is slightly shallower than the breaststroke turn, but is like it in all other ways (Fig. 8.8). Both hands touch the wall simultaneously as the whole body stretches toward the end of the pool (the head may, however, dip below the surface in butterfly). The hands, one at a time, then leave the wall as the legs tuck under the body and come around toward the wall. Note that the feet once they are ready to push off are slightly higher on the wall than in the breaststroke turn, but that the shoulders are still low in the water as the legs come around in preparation for the push off and stretch off the wall.

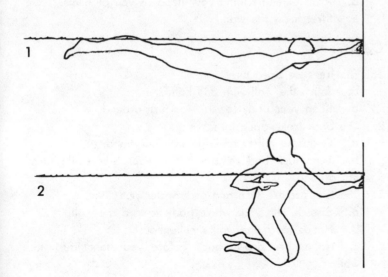

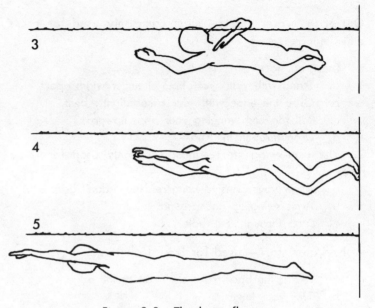

Figure 8.8 **The butterfly turn**

## CHAPTER SUMMARY

### Starts

Out-of-the-water starts are used for freestyle, breaststroke, and butterfly.

An in-the-water start is used for backstroke.

All starts should be fast and streamlined.

Out-of-the-water starts—most commonly used for races other than relays.

1. The grab start.
    a. Stand with your feet about shoulder width apart.
    b. Grab the edge with your knees slightly bent.
    c. Roll forward swinging your arms upward.
    d. Drop through the "hole."
2. The arm-swing start—most commonly used for relay races.
    a. Allow your arms to hang relaxed—don't grab.
    b. Arms swing up and around.
    c. Drop through the "hole."

In-the-water start—used for backstroke.

    a. Grasp the backstroke start rail or the edge.
    b. Tuck your knees.
    c. Pull your body up.
    d. Throw your arms to the sides as you lift your chin.

Turns

Flip Turns.

1. The freestyle flip turn—resembles a somersault.
    a. Chin drops.
    b. One or both arms push toward your hips.

    c. Feet come over.
    d. Body twist.
    e. Hands leave the wall before your feet touch.
    f. Stretch off the wall.
2. The backstroke flip turn—a "spin" turn.
    a. Fingers point downward and your arm is nearly straight when your hand touches the wall.
    b. Knees tuck.
    c. Head and hips exchange places as your hand leaves the wall.
    d. Arms extend behind your head as you push off.
    e. Stretch off the wall.

Open Turns

1. The freestyle open turn.
    a. Touch the wall with one hand.
    b. Keep your body low as you turn around.
2. The backstroke open turn.
    a. Grab the gutter or edge with one hand.
    b. Legs tuck and remain below your hips while turning around.
3. The breaststroke turn and underwater pull
    a. Stretch with your whole body toward the wall.
    b. Hands touch the wall simultaneously.
    c. Hands are drawn back before your feet touch the wall.

d.  Head is slightly lower than the hips on the push-off and stretch off the wall.

e.  One underwater pull and kick can follow each turn and start.

4.  The butterfly turn

a.  Stretch toward the wall.

b.  Hands touch the wall simultaneously.

c.  Legs tuck under the body to come around.

d.  Feet are slightly higher on the wall than in the breaststroke.

e.  Keep your body low as you turn around.

# 9. *Some Obstacles to Swimming— And Their Solutions*

Once you have spent enough time in the water to have become reasonably proficient at one or more strokes and to have experimented with some of the suggested training methods, you have perhaps encountered some physical discomforts or inconveniences that led you to wonder if you should temporarily alter or discontinue your training. Or possibly it would be more accurate to say that once you have lived through the months or years it took you to gain sound stroke mechanics and an ability to do some kind of interval training, you have also been exposed to a good deal of the wear and tear and hazards of everyday living which at times caused you either to stop swimming for a time or to wonder if you should. Perhaps you have experienced some pain or restricted movement from a past or recent injury, or some shoulder or knee pain after a strenuous swimming workout, or perhaps suddenly, just when your swimming seemed to be going exceptionally well, you began to notice that your pulse rate after a hard swimming series did not drop as rapidly as before. Or maybe you have had, or will have, reason to wonder about swimming after illness or surgery, or during pregnancy.

My point is simply that all of us are subject to some stresses and strains not only in swimming, but also in "real life," and all of this is likely at times to make swimming difficult, yet at the same time all the more beneficial in most cases. In the following sections, I discuss some of the more common obstacles you might encounter, either as a result of your swimming, or in spite of it, and present what I feel is a positive approach to each one.

## RANGE-OF-MOTION LIMITATIONS

Any physiological state that causes a restriction of normal movement would be considered a range-of-motion limitation. Such limitations can be classified in one of two ways: those not caused by swimming; and those caused by swimming.

The reasons for range of motion limitations not caused by swimming vary from the stiffness resulting from a long history of sedentary life, or too much garden work the day before, to the permanent disability of a stroke, accident, or birth defect. But no matter what the reason, in all but a very few cases about which your doctor could advise you, gentle exercise in the water to the affected area will increase circulation which in turn can help mobility.

In-the-water exercise, in addition to gently increasing circulation in problem areas, is also an excellent way to massage weak or injured muscles back into activity, since water is dense enough to ripple your skin and outer muscle layer as you move forward against the resistance of the water.

In comparison to those caused by other sports, range-of-motion limitations caused by swimming are relatively few. After all, swimming injuries tend to come gradually (giving you time to detect the early symptoms), since sudden jarring pressures on joints and muscles and risk of falling are non-existent. But swimming, like any sport, does stress certain areas of your body more than others, and because of the repetitive nature of your movements when swimming, some pain and restriction of movement can result if you are not careful.

In swimming, the area where stress is most often felt is in the shoulder region. The reason for this is that when you extend your arm over your head (or in front of it, as is the case when you are in a swimming position), the inner layer of muscles of the shoulder joint called the "rotator cuff" impinges upon the bony acromion (the lateral extension of the shoulder blade). Also, some of the tendons in the shoulder area, such as the suraspinatus tendon and the biceps tendon, undergo considerable strain.[20]

If this strain does cause tenderness in the shoulder region, you should first have someone carefully check your stroke technique for possible defects that could increase strain. You must also see that you do not develop a faulty stroke pattern which will place undue stress on another area that is not used to high strain.

Other areas that are sometimes affected by stress, but much less often than the shoulder, are the knee and the ankle and foot. Knee pain is usually from the "medial ligament," which undergoes stress during the whip-like action of a properly executed breaststroke kick.[21] Ankle and foot limitations can result from the extreme flexion that the ankle joint and toes must undergo when resistance presses the toes down during the propulsive phase of the freestyle, backstroke, and butterfly kicks. Also for this reason, swim fins, which exaggerate this flexion should be eliminated from your training and only gradually reinstated if any tenderness develops.

But, as mentioned, swimming injuries of any kind tend to happen gradually, with the pain coming at first only after hard swimming. Thus if you become aware of pain in any of the key areas I have mentioned, you can adjust your training load on that particular area in order to greatly reduce the risk of further pain or range of motion limitations.

Preventing stress pains, however, is an easier task than dealing with pain once it occurs. The following are some steps you can take to help prevent swimming stress point injuries.

1.   Begin your training program gradually, particularly if you have not exercised in several months or years. (See Chapter 2 for more specific suggestions on how to begin.)
2.   Do five to ten minutes of easy warmup swimming before you begin the strenuous portion of your training session.
3.   Take several minutes at the end of your practice session to do some easy loosen-up swimming.
4.   Pay close attention to proper stroke technique.
5.   Avoid sudden jerking movements in the water, or when entering and leaving the water.
6.   Do some stretching exercises each day to increase your range of motion (see Chapter 10 for specific suggestions).
7.   Consult a coach or physician if you feel pain in any of the stress-point areas.

In short, avoiding any unnecessary strain and keeping your muscles loose is the key. The warm-up swimming, particularly, is crucial. You may even wish to do mini-warm-ups for specific areas of the body, as needed, throughout your practice session. For example, if you have been doing a long kicking series, you might want to loosen up your arms a bit before beginning to swim again, or if you have been pulling, your legs may need warming up. By doing this, you will also eliminate the uncomfortable tight feeling of suddenly straining muscles that have been at rest.

In conclusion, I would say that range of motion limitations should, with a coach's or physician's consent (depending upon the level of the affliction), be treated with gentle in-the-water exercise to aid mobility. Abstinence from swimming or water exercise should be considered only as a last resort, and all precautions should be taken to see that an injury does not become so serious that time out of the water will be required.

## TENDONITIS

Tendonitis simply refers to inflammation of the soft connective tissue of the muscles. Because tendons and ligaments have a lesser blood supply than muscles or organs, they heal more slowly once inflammation occurs.

In swimmers, this ailment can affect the shoulder region and cause severe range-of-motion limitations and lost swimming time if precautions are not taken. One approach to preventing tendonitis or relieving it once it sets in, is to employ gentle exercise as long as this does not aggravate further pain. Water exercise is excellent, but can be supplemented with some exercises that make use of gravity and must therefore be done on land.

These exercises were brought to my attention in the following article which I have included below by Nancy Ridout, a serious Masters swimmer and shoulder pain sufferer. After reading the article, I discussed the prescribed exercises with Patsi Sinnott, a registered physical therapist at the University of California Medical Center in San Francisco, who suggested that if the exercises were performed in a bent-over, right-angle position then gravity could assist some of the movements, thereby minimizing strain to the fullest.[22] When I mentioned this to Nancy, she agreed that this would indeed be a better position than standing erect.

Nancy Ridout, age 36 and mother of two, from Novato, California is one of the top Masters swimmers nationwide in her age group today. She is a national record holder in the 50 and 100 yard freestyle, as well as a Masters All-American. In 1977 she won the women's Outstanding Pacific Association Masters Swimmer of the Year award, having been chosen from among nearly five hundred swimmers in Northern California.

## "RELIEF FOR SHOULDER PAIN OR TENDONITIS"[23]
### by Nancy Ridout

*Many of us have experienced the sensations of severe shoulder pain or tendonitis. About the only advice given to its sufferers is complete rest from whatever activity produced it and/or a shot of cortisone.*

*Having experienced tendonitis myself on several occasions, the latest, three weeks before the Short Course Masters Nationals, neither of the above was what I wanted at that point.*

*Don Schwartz, the former coach of the Marin Aquatic Club, gave me three exercises developed by Bob Fuller, a registered physical therapist and owner of "Bob Fuller's Conditioning and Therapy" in San Rafael, California. I have used them since the first occurrence several years ago and I can say without hesitation — they work!*

*Pain from tendonitis is experienced as slight-to-severe pain in the shoulder joint. It occurs most often in the shoulder opposite the breathing arm (since this arm in many cases reaches further under the body), and it may extend down the arm and/or down the back.*

*It limits our range of movement. Attempting across-the-body movements with that arm becomes painful. Weakness* occurs when reaching the wrong way to lift or hold something. A warmup of 500 yards or more is needed before one can feel strength or power from that shoulder.

Man was made to propel himself by his legs, not his arms. That is why stress can occur here when we increase our yardage suddenly, work hard or harder with hand paddles, throw a ball more than we're used to, play more badminton, tennis, and so forth.

The exercises are as follows:

1.   Backward arm circles as in straight arm backstroke, one arm at a time. If you can't get all the way around, go as far as you can. Repeat circles for one minute.
2.   Forward arm circles with a straight arm, one arm at a time. If you can't get all the way around, go as far as you can. Repeat circles for one minute.
3.   Arm straight out to the side at a right angle with your trunk, palm down. Swing your arm down, across your body, and up as far as possible on the other side; then back again. Repeat for one minute.

All three exercises should be done with straight but not stiff arms, using gentle rather than vigorous arm movements.

The exercises should be done in succession: number 1 for one minutes, then number 2 for one minute, and then number 3 for one minute. For severe impairment, three times, for a total of nine minutes three times per day.

It shouldn't take much more than a week to be rid of the pain. However, in one case I know of, it took two weeks. After the tendonitis is relieved, a maintenance schedule of once per day for nine minutes should be enough.

The exercises, though they may seem simple or unrelated, do work. If they are done properly and often enough, they will not only clear up the condition but keep it from recurring. And you don't have to stop training!

The tendency is to stop the exercises when the pain is gone. It happens to everyone. However, a daily maintenance schedule will keep you free from tendonitis in the shoulder and save you many problems.

## STIFFNESS AND SORENESS

Some stiffness and soreness are to be expected if you work hard enough and long enough each day at your swimming to bring and maintain your heart rate at a fitness inducing level. But here again, the object is to keep soreness under control so that it does not interfere with normal range of motion or cause loss of practice time. Physiologically, stiffness is simply a mild case of soreness and both are caused by the buildup of waste products such as carbon dioxide and lactic acid in the muscles.

How do you minimize this buildup? First of all, if you exercise regularly, *all* of the functions of your muscles will increase in efficiency, including their ability to rid themselves of waste products. So keep your training load fairly constant, or increase gradually if you want to do more, and ease back into the routine if your training happens to be interrupted for more than a week or two.

Second, a proper swim-down at the end of your training session will stretch out still partially contracted muscles, which otherwise will tend to retain waste products. Stretching on land using the exercises described in Chapter 10 can also be helpful in relaxing your muscles after strenuous swimming.

Third, you should train with the realization that muscle soreness is closely connected with muscle contraction; the more intense the contraction, the more quickly soreness will develop. You can surely attest to this fact if you think back to the last time you nearly had a dangerous fall, but made a perhaps none too glamorous save by suddenly bracing yourself, and the next day you were so sore you wished you had gone ahead and fallen since no injury could be worse than the pain you were already feeling. My point is that sudden short bursts of intense swimming are far more likely to cause stiffness and soreness than moderate amounts of distance swimming because muscle contraction is greater in sprints. So vary your training and if you feel stiffness or mild soreness the day after a particular training session, emphasize middle or longer distances at the next practice.

For severe soreness, ice should be used during the first hour or two after the stress-causing activity, then heat should be applied.

## OVERTRAINING

Overtraining occurs when the body suffers a failing adaptation to the stress of swimming. And it can happen to a person at any level of fitness, especially since overtraining can be the result of an accumulation of stresses from all aspects of life combined, not just from the physical exertion of swimming. This is why an adult, who must stand up under job pressures, demanding family obligations, or financial responsibilities, can as easily become a victim of overtraining as a high school or college swimmer.

The higher your level of training, however, the finer the line between improving your fitness and tearing your body down to the point that no positive physiological results can take place. Coaches of world class swimmers, for example, must push athletes to the very peak of their capabilities, while always keeping a careful watch for even the most minute signs of failing adaptation. Some coaches even have their swimmers take daily blood analysis tests during periods of unusually strenuous training so that early signs of over-training such as electrolyte imbalance or glycogen depletion can be detected even before the swimmer notices any symptoms. Electrolyte imbalance contributes to cramps, depression and general fatigue. Glycogen depletion also leads to decreased performance and, according to Dr. Stuart Bergman, can occur if you train vigorously when your glycogen level is already low because of previous training.[24]

Many other body functions are affected as well by over-training, but the main point is that stress must decrease in order for recovery to take place once the syndrome of failing adaptation begins. This can be difficult if outside stresses such as lack of sleep, worry, poor diet, or recent illness are also contributing to fatigue, and frustrating if a significant loss of training time is necessary. So be alert to the earliest signs of overtraining.

Dr. Paul Hutinger believes that the following are clues to detecting overtraining.

1.   Insomnia — which can lead to further deterioration of the body since without sleep the swimmer suffers greater stress at the next training session.

2.   Awakening at night from being hot and sweaty — a condition that may last ten to thirty minutes.

3.   A higher-than-your-usual basal heart rate — especially one that remains high for several days.

4.   Irritability and sudden anger.[25]

Other symptoms which could be signs of overtraining, according to Herbert A. deVries, include:

1.   A working heart rate which does not drop as rapidly as usual after hard repeat swims.

2.   A sudden, unexplainable weight loss.

3.   A sudden increase in your resting blood pressure.[26]

You should, however, monitor any such findings more than once to be sure that they are accurate before you draw conclusions.

But, take heart, swimming has some advantages over terrestrial sports when it comes to overtraining in that when overstress begins to take hold, the evaporative cooling effect of water on the skin greatly reduces the risk of heat exhaustion and heat stroke. Also, in any sports that require balance or quick, precise movements, such as tennis, racquet ball, squash, gymnastics, or sports that demand a fair amount of running, such as jogging, long-distance running, basketball, and soccer, the danger of falling or of injury to joints and muscles rises greatly when the participant becomes over-trained. The chance of injury during swimming, on the other hand, is quite low to begin with, and it rises much less sharply during periods when the athlete is overtrained. Fall-ing or bumping into objects at high speed is not possible when swimming, nor are sudden extreme pressures or wrenching movements, because of the dense, protective consistency of water. (This is the same protection the body provides for babies before they are born.)

## SWIMMING TO RECOVER FROM INJURY

Perhaps the most dramatic difference between exercising on land and exercising in water is that water assumes much of the weight bearing function that the body must perform when surrounded by air. This makes swimming particularly advan-tageous as an aid in healing muscle and joint injuries which require exercise.

The lower extremities of the body, especially, can function far sooner after injury and with considerably less effort in the water where the body weight to be borne is next to none. And in serious injury or even birth defect cases in which a person is incapable of supporting himself without help on land, he may well be quite capable of independent support and movement in the water. This I would imagine to be a thrill beyond words. In fact, I have heard of cases in which severely handicapped persons were able to rehabilitate their whole attitude toward themselves, their loved ones, and their jobs after discovering new freedom and self-confidence in the water.

But exercise in the water is an ideal way to bring all parts of the body, not just the lower extremities, back into full activity. Swimming, in fact, aside from gradually strength-ening damaged muscles, can help break down adhesions in connective tissue during the healing process. Moreover, according to Dr. Paul Hutinger, while heart attack, arthritis, joint problems, hypoglycemia, diabetes, as well as previous surgery or injuries may limit your swimming, you need not (unless specifically recommended by a physician), and in-deed should not, eliminate swimming from your daily rou-tine. In fact, you stand an excellent chance of increasing your limits if, with proper medical supervision, you keep it up.[27]

If you should suffer an injury to an arm or leg which does require complete rest, however, you can capitalize on the miracle of your natural buoyancy in the water and keep right on swimming. How? A kickboard can be used to isolate an injured arm or shoulder, while, with slightly more difficulty in turns, a pull buoy can do the same for a leg or foot injury. I have even seen swimmers with fractures who obtained fibreglass waterproof casts so they wouldn't miss swimming.

## SWIMMING WITH THE BODY CHANGES CAUSED BY PREGNANCY

Although swimming with additional weight in the pelvic region may seem awkward to you (especially if you do flip turns), obstetricians generally agree that pregnant women, like everyone else, should participate in physical activity and obtain the benefits of fitness. The only caution is that you should participate only as long as you feel comfortable.

According to Jill Kelly, in her article on the subject in *Ms Magazine*, danger to the fetus is minimal because the uterus is so well protected within a water bag, just as you are guarded against the forces of high speed and gravity when you are contained in a swimming pool.[28] And precisely because water is nature's own most perfect protection for mother and child, combined with the fact that water is an excellent weight bearing medium, swimming is the exercise best suited to pregnancy. More specifically, an unborn baby is protected by its mother's water from the dangers of being shaken or moved suddenly, while the mother's pelvic ligaments are unburdened by the water she swims in.

Another reason why swimming is preferable to other forms of physical activity (although some kind of exercise is far better than none) is that the risk of injury is low and the risk of falling is nonexistent (except when getting into and out of the pool, a maneuver over which you should exercise the greatest caution). In sports that require balance and coordination, such as tennis or gymnastics, your changed body weight can affect your performance and increase your chances of injury. For this reason, obstetricians consistently recommend that during pregnancy you continue with physical activities that you are used to, rather than taking up new ones, so that you can more easily compensate for altered weight. In sports that require twisting, such as golf or field events, changed weight can cause back problems, especially in the late stages of pregnancy.

When exercising during pregnancy, however, always remember that you should do so, as mentioned, only as long as you are comfortable, and according to Ms. only as long as you do not experience anything out of the ordinary such as pains or spotting.[29] But other than this, after talking with several pregnant swimmers about what their doctors had to say concerning swimming during pregnancy, as well as three doctors, I know of no other restrictions on swimming, except that you should be careful getting into and out of the pool. All of the athletes I talked to were told they could return to swimming after pregnancy once bleeding had stopped.

Medical opinion on the matter of swimming and pregnancy, however, seems to have changed over the years, at least in some cases. One woman who had been pregnant eleven years earlier reported that her doctor had advised refraining from swimming for six weeks before delivery because water with its impurities could conceivably enter the birth canal if the cervix was partially dilated. When I asked Dr. Harold Dennis for his opinion on this, he said that he didn't think it possible for water to seep in, but he had heard of doctors recommending that their patients avoid baths and swimming in the late stages of pregnancy because of the risk of falling when getting into and out of the tub or pool.[30]

But today the universal opinion is that exercise is good — even during pregnancy. Exercise improves all of the many physiological responses of the body, says Dr. Dorothy Harris, director of Pennsylvania State University's Center for Women and Sport; particularly relevant to pregnancy are circulation, which, of course, is crucial to the growth of the fetus, and muscle tone, which plays an important role in labor and delivery.[31]

One last bit of information that I came upon when talking to pregnant swimmers and that I should pass on to you, is that the lycra bathing suits for racing have another advantage. Apparently the large sizes make exceptionally comfortable attire for swimming during pregnancy because of the extreme elasticity of the fabric.

Susan Jones Roy, age 30, from Cupertino, California, was a member of the 1968 U.S. Olympic Team and is still going strong with her swimming, despite the demands of her year-old son. She is presently a national record holder in the 200 meter breaststroke and is coaching the Alpine Masters swimmers in Portola Valley.

## "SWIMMING THROUGH A PREGNANCY"
### by Susan Jones Roy

*After ten years of competitive AAU swimming in California, a berth on the U.S. Olympic team, a world record in the breaststroke, and three years in the Masters program, I was not ready to give up my swimming when I became pregnant. And I was, quite frankly, threatened at the thought that my swimming should come to a stop. But I soon discovered, to my great relief, that I did not have to stop, or even change my swimming habits to any great extent.*

*While running in the middle and late stages of pregnancy*

can be uncomfortable and put great strain on the joints and lower back, I found that I experienced no strain whatsoever in any part of my body when swimming during any phase of my pregnancy. As a matter of fact, because of the water's ability to provide support, my swimming session became a time when I could relax and most thoroughly enjoy a "weightless" feeling.

But just as important is the fact that through swimming during my pregnancy, I was able to maintain my stamina and fitness, both of which I feel were helpful to me in the strenuous task of child delivery. Also, with the help of my conditioning I made a rapid recovery after delivery.

## Quantity and Quality

In determining how much and how intensely I should swim during my pregnancy, I followed the rule, "do what feels comfortable." And I found that due to my previous training I was able to maintain my three workouts per week of 2000 meters each throughout my entire pregnancy. But I will advise others that if swimming is a new exercise for you at the time of your pregnancy, begin gradually and don't over-do it.

Although the quantity of swimming I did during each workout did not vary, I did discover that as my pregnancy progressed, my 2000 meters took increasingly longer to complete. During the first three months, thirty minutes was sufficient, but by the last three months, I needed forty to fifty minutes.

The frequency of my workouts, also, did not vary. I made it a point to swim at least three times a week, and I tried to spread my workouts evenly throughout the week so that I would never go more than two days in a row without training. I firmly believe that one needs just as much exercise during pregnancy as at other times, and it seems obstetricians generally agree that swimming throughout pregnancy is an excellent way to exercise.

The quality of my workouts, however, did change when I became pregnant. I avoided strenuous workouts not only because of the discomfort they caused, but also because a growing fetus puts added stress on a woman's cardiovascular system. So I concentrated on doing repeat swims at slower speeds, and I enjoyed long distance stroke work.

## Stroke Modifications

Although I was pleasantly surprised to discover how comfortably I could perform the four basic strokes during my pregnancy, I found certain stroke modifications necessary as I grew larger.

Freestyle.

*Because of my increased volume in the water, I became more buoyant, which in turn caused my head position to rise, restricting shoulder rotation to some extent. Therefore, to compensate, my underwater pull became deeper and wider. I also stopped doing flip turns when tucking began to be uncomfortable.*

Backstroke.

*This stroke was by far the most enjoyable stroke for me in my newly buoyant state. I seemed to float quite naturally in the water, therefore stroking and kicking were easier.*

Breaststroke.

*Breaststroke was also quite comfortable for me. But I found that to compensate for the changed balance of my body in the water, I had to pull deeper and wider.*

Butterfly.

*This was the only stroke that I eventually discontinued. At around the fourth month, butterfly became just plain awkward. I experienced an uncomfortable pulling sensation on my stomach muscles when I pushed my arms out of the water for recovery.*

## Types of Workouts

*With an eye toward moderate exercise, I did workouts like those listed below at various stages of my pregnancy.*

*Workout 1 (first trimester of pregnancy):*
    *400 meters freestyle with fins*
    *5 × 100 meters individual medley (25 meters of each stroke) with one minute rest between each 100 meters*
    *2 × 200 meters kick*
    *300 meters freestyle pull*
    *8 × 50 meters breaststroke or butterfly*

*Workout 2 (second trimester of pregnancy):*
    *200 meters freestyle pull*
    *200 meters freestyle kick*
    *200 meters freestyle swim with fins*
    *2 × 300 meters individual medley (no butterfly)*
    *5 × 100 meters freestyle with 30 seconds rest between each 100 meters*
    *300 meters easy kick*

*Workout 3 (third trimester of pregnancy):*
    *500 meters freestyle with fins*
    *500 meters kick any stroke*
    *500 meters backstroke with fins*
    *500 meters breaststroke*

## Competition During Pregnancy

*I like to swim in competition a few times a year, and during the fourth month of my pregnancy I competed in a local Masters meet in which I swam well with no side effects. Here again, I followed the rule "do what feels comfortable," so I avoided certain strokes and distances, but enjoyed the events I did swim.*

*In short, I was able to enjoy my pregnancy and quickly regain my figure afterwards by staying healthy and fit through swimming.*

## CHAPTER SUMMARY

### Range-of-Motion Limitations

Range-of-motion limitation is physiologically restricted movement.

1. Those not caused by swimming—the treatment in most cases is gentle exercise in the water.
2. Those caused by swimming.

Chance of injury is considerably lower than in other sports.

There are no jarring pressures on the joints and muscles.

The risk of falling in nonexistent.

Key pressure points are the shoulder region, the knee, and the ankle and foot.

To prevent swimming stress point injuries:

   a.  Begin training gradually.
   b.  Do a warmup
   c.  Loosen-up after hard swimming.
   d.  Watch stroke technique.
   e.  Avoid sudden movements.
   f.  Stretch.
   g.  If you have pain, see a coach or physician.

Once injury occurs the treatment is most often gentle exercise.

### Tendonitis

Tendonitis is inflammation of the soft connective tissue of the muscles.

The treatment in all but the most severe cases is gentle exercise in the water and out.

Out-of-the-water exercises:

1. Backward arm circles.
2. Forward arm circles.
3. Arm swing.

### Stiffness and Soreness

Stiffness and soreness are caused by the buildup of waste products in the muscles.

Some stiffness and soreness are to be expected in a rigorous swimming program.

You can minimize stiffness and soreness by:

1. Exercising regularly.
2. Loosening up properly.
3. Stretching.

For severe soreness ice and later heat should be used.

## Overtraining

Overtraining occurs when the body suffers failing adaptation to stress.

Stress must decrease in order for recovery to take place. Signs of overtraining are:

1. Insomnia.
2. Awakening hot and sweaty at night.
3. An increased basal heart rate.
4. Irritability and sudden anger.

Possible signs of overtraining:

1. A working heart rate which is reluctant to drop.
2. Sudden weight loss.
3. An increase in resting blood pressure.

The chance of heat exhaustion and injury because of overtraining is quite low in swimming.

## Swimming to Recover from Injury

That water can carry body weight is crucial to the therapeutic efficiency of swimming.

Also, the density of water makes it an excellent medium for gently exercising muscles and joints back into mobility.

## Swimming with the Body Changes
## Caused by Pregnancy

Pregnant women, like everyone else, should exercise.

Swimming is the exercise best suited to pregnancy because there is the least chance of injury to mother and child.

You should exercise great caution, however, when getting into and out of the pool.

Slight modifications can be made in stroke technique to accommodate the body's extra bulk.

# 10. Building Flexibility and Strength—"Swimming" Without Swimming

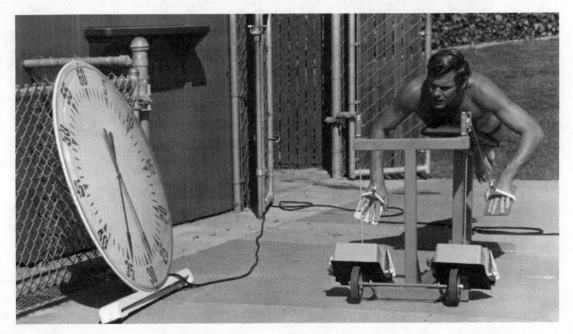

*A*fter your swimming program is well under way, you will probably be interested in building flexibility and strength away from the pool, or at least in ways other than swimming back and forth using the four principal strokes. There are several reasons for this interest: (1) you feel that if you had more flexibility and strength you could swim more efficiently; (2) you cannot always make it to the pool and you wonder what you can do to help your swimming on such occasions; and (3) you would like to add some variety to your exercise routine. You should realize, however, that none of the exercises discussed here contribute as significantly to cardiovascular fitness as the continuous movement of swimming. Therefore, they should not take the place of swimming, except for brief periods if it is total fitness you desire. Rather, the exercises should be considered as supplements to your program. So the following exercises are presented with the assumption that swimming is still your number one physical activity, but that you would like to do something more than swim to improve your swimming as well as your sense of well-being.

Perhaps the easiest additional activity to fit into your schedule is stretching since it doesn't require equipment and can be done anywhere, at any time — while waiting for a bus, or watching TV, or better yet, instead of a martini after work (and the effects are more exhilarating to be sure). And besides, stretching is an excellent means of increasing flexibility.

What does "flexibility" mean? Flexibility is simply the range of motion of a joint which, according to Counsilman, is limited by bone structure and muscle elasticity, both of which vary greatly from person to person.[32] Bone structure, of course, cannot be changed, but muscle elasticity can improve with stretching.

Why is flexibility important? In short, the answer is that flexibility is the foundation of all movement. Therefore, if you have developed your flexibility through stretching, your movements will be easier (thanks to increased range of motion) and your resilience to soreness and injury will be greater. Stretching is also, according to Bob Anderson, author of *Stretching*, an important factor in priming our bodies to experience the full joy of physical activity.[33]

If you are still not quite convinced about the merits of stretching, or if you question whether you really have time for it, let me appeal to your vanity and ask you to consider that increased flexibility can lend supple beauty and grace to your style as you glide down the pool because movements will be easier for you. In other words, stretching will make your stroke more aesthetic in the sense that you will appear to be moving forward with less effort. And indeed you will be doing just that because the more flexible your joints are, the less energy you need to move them. It follows, then, that if you expend the same amount of effort after increased flexibility as you did before it, you will swim faster with no increased energy output. Moreover, a stretched muscle contracts faster, which will also help your speed.

How often should stretching be done? A good rule to follow is always to stretch before or after you exercise (preferably both), and any other time you like. Unlike strength building activities, you can never do too much, and you may find that you can stretch out the minor aches, pains, and tensions that daily life brings about. The reason I suggest stretching both before and after exercise is that it's useful as a warmup for strenuous activity, and even more useful as a means of relaxing muscles that may still be in a semicontracted state from exertion. Furthermore, you can even stretch while in the water to relieve any stiffness, side aches, or cramps you may experience.

Although swimming itself increases flexibility, which unfortunately tends to decline with age, you can significantly increase your improvement in joint mobility by regularly doing the following flexibility exercises. Try to relax as much as possible while stretching, and remember it's never too late to start.

## STRETCHING EXERCISES

Some of the following exercises I have invented, while others I have observed in exercise classes. For still others, I have Bob Anderson to thank.

### Shoulders

1.   Forward arm circles. Swing one arm forward in circles, keeping it straight. Repeat with the other arm.
2.   Backward arm circles. Swing one arm backward in circles, keeping it straight. Repeat with the other arm.
3.   Forward and back arm swings. Swing your straight arms toward one another at chest level until they cross, then swing them as far back behind you as you can.
4.   Partner arm stretches. Put your straight arms behind you with your palms facing out and your thumbs up. Have a partner push and hold your arms as close together as possible without giving you discomfort, and hold.
5.   Chicken wings. Raise one arm directly above your head, allowing your forearm to hang down your back. Push the elbow down behind your head with your other hand and hold. Repeat with the other arm.
6.   "N" stretches. Raise one arm directly above your head,

allowing your forearm to hang down your back. Bring your other arm around behind you, forearm against your side, and grasp one hand with the other (or go as close as you can) and hold.

7. Arms-over-head stretches. From a standing position, clasp your hands behind your back and bend over, bringing your straight arms up over your head as far as possible and hold. Also keep your knees straight.

8. Towel stretches. With your arms in front of you, grasp a towel with your hands more than shoulder width apart. Rotate your straight arms backward until your hands are behind your hips. Return to the starting position. As you become more flexible, move your hands closer together.

## Legs and Ankles

1. Toe touches. Keeping your knees straight, bend over and stretch as far as you can, touching your toes or the floor, if possible, and hold.

2. Plantar sits. Kneel with the soles of your feet up and sit back on your heels. Using your hands for balance, raise your knees as far as you can and hold.

3. Push-ups on the wall. Place your palms against a wall and your feet, toes pointing forward, 2 to 3 feet from the wall (depending upon your height). Keeping your heels on the floor, bend your elbows so your head nearly touches the wall. Return to the starting position. Also try placing your toes on top of a brick, or a thick book for greater stretching.

4. Hurdle stretches. Sit on the floor with one leg extended straight in front of you, toes pointing up. Your other leg, which is bent, forms a right angle with your straight leg. Try to touch your forehead to your straight knee and hold. Repeat with the other leg.

5. Breaststroke squats. Kneel with your feet turned out. Sit back as far as possible and hold, using your hands for balance.

6. Rocker Squats. Squat down with one leg extended straight out to the side, toes pointing up, your other leg bent with your foot flat on the floor. Rock from side to side alternately bending and extending each leg.

7. Yoga Sits. Sit with the soles of your feet together, your feet as close to your body as possible. Bend forward trying to touch your forehead to your instep and hold.[34]

## Spine and Abdomen

1. Back stretchers. Kneel with the soles of your feet up and sit back on top of your heels. Lean back and try to touch your head to the floor.

2. Front extension. Lie down on your stomach and clasp your hands behind your head. Lift your shoulders as high off the floor as possible and hold.

3. Airplane twists. Lie down on your back with your arms straight out to the sides. Bring your left foot, leaving the right foot where it is and keeping both legs straight, over to touch your right hand. Repeat with your right foot.

4. Rolls back and forth. Lie on your back with your hands at your sides. Bring your legs, knees straight, up over your head until your toes touch the floor. Also come down with straight legs.[35]

5. Side stretches. Stand with your arms extended overhead, hands clasped with palms facing each other. Lean to the right side as far as possible and hold. Repeat to the left side.[36]

6. Speed skaters. Stand with your feet shoulder width apart and lean forward, bending at the waist. Extend your arms to the sides and swing one arm under your body to the right and the other arm over your body to the left, twisting as far as possible and keeping your arms opposite one another. Repeat on the other side.

7. Jackknife sit-ups. Lie on your back with your hands at your sides. Lift your feet with straight legs and pointed toes, 12 to 18 inches (about 30 to 45 cm.) off the floor and touch your toes with your hands.

8. Plantar push-ups. Place your palms on the floor at shoulder width and extend your body so that the tops of your feet rest on the floor and your arms are straight. Bend your arms, keeping your body straight, until it comes close to the floor, but does not touch it. Return to the starting position.

9. Heel raisers. Standing, raise your heels as far as possible off the floor. Return your heels to the floor.

For all of the preceding exercises which indicate that you should "hold" a certain position, try to hold for 5 to 10 seconds or more without bouncing or moving. I would also suggest that you do five to ten repetitions of each exercise per session.

Flexibility exercises are especially useful when you're also following a program of strength building exercises, which could cause soreness if you don't properly stretch out and relax your muscles afterward. In fact, the maximum benefits of strength building can only be achieved if flexibility is built into the joints over which these muscles work.

But strength building, like stretching, must not become a substitute for swimming, except for occasional instances when training in the pool is impossible. Rather it should be a supplement, since strength training will not substantially contribute to your cardiovascular fitness.

There are many methods of strength building, and the cost

of apparatus for them can range from a few dollars to several thousand dollars. And for some types of strength training, you need no equipment at all. So, what's the difference, you ask, between the benefits you will derive from an expensive piece of equipment as opposed to an inexpensive one, or from strength building without equipment? The short and simple answer to this question is that some of the more costly devices can offer you a method of training that is highly specific not only to the sport of swimming, but also the particular movements required in individual strokes and in starts and turns. On the other hand less costly devices usually offer a method of increasing your strength in general. But to give you a more complete answer, you must first understand some important concepts.

First of all, realize that the methods of overloading muscles in order to build strength are basically of two types: "static," or those that require muscles to exert force, which results in little or no movement, such as force against a stationary object; and "dynamic," or those that require the muscles to exert force through the entire range of motion of a joint.

Static strength training through the use of isometric (without motion) exercises can lead to a significant increase in strength, and it has the distinct advantages that it requires very little if any equipment, very little space, and no special facilities. But at the same time static exercise cannot relate as efficiently to a motor function like swimming as does dynamic exercise, which itself requires motion. In other words, strength training which demands movement best prepares you for an activity which also demands movement. Keep in mind, however, that static training is still preferable to no strength training at all. The following are a few simple isometric exercises that relate well to swimming. (Perhaps you can make up some of your own, too.)

## ISOMETRIC EXERCISES

1.  Arm press-up with straight arms. Lie on your back with your arms extended behind your head, elbows straight. Place your hands, palms up, against the bottom of the sofa. Press up and hold.
2.  Arm Press-Up with Bent Arms. Lie on your back with your arms, at right angles, extended behind your head. Proceed as in number 1.
3.  Wall press. Lie on your back with your forearms and palms against a wall, elbows pointing upward. Press against the wall with your hands and hold.

4. Leg lift. Lie on your back. Raise your legs, with straight knees, 6 inches off the floor and hold.
5. Ankle press-up. Sit with your knees straight and your toes pointed and tucked under a bed. Press with the tops of your feet against the bottom of the bed and hold.
6. Table press-up. Standing, bend forward with straight legs, and place your palms, hands behind you, under a table top. Press up with your hands and hold.
7. Table press-down. Kneeling, press down on a table top with your elbows bent at right angles and at the same levels as your hands and shoulders.
8. Doorway press. Stand in a doorway and with straight arms press your hands out as far from your body as possible and hold.

For the above exercises I would recommend holding each position for 15 seconds, five to ten times per session.

One very important use of isometric exercises that should not be overlooked is in strengthening muscles in areas of the body where the full range of motion necessary to perform movement cannot be achieved. Rehabilitation, then, from many kinds of injury or illness, and even from some hereditary defects, can come about through the use of static training.

Dynamic strength training, however, has certain points in its favor that relate to the efficiency of building the most applicable kind of strength in the shortest period of time per session. As mentioned, static training builds the kind of strength ideally suited to activities which require power but little or no movement, whereas dynamic training applies best to motor performance.

The concept of training with motion can be broken down still further. To avoid a highly technical explanation, let me simply say that motion in strength training can be slow or fast and that the resistance against which you work can be high or low; all of these factors yield different physiological results. For example, a weight lifter, a football player, and a swimmer will all do different types of strength training because the demands of their sports are very different. Each will do specific training for his or her own activity.

How will the swimmer train? According to Dr. James Counsilman, speed is important in strength training if your muscles are to develop the qualities that will be most useful during swimming — namely the ability to contract quickly, and the ability to maintain strength over a period of time.[37] No one exercise is superior in developing both of these qualities but a combination of exercises can induce both.

So that you will know what kinds of exercises bring about speed in a muscle and which bring endurance, let us look at Counsilman's "Three R's of Exercise":

1. Resistance. This is the amount of weight against which the muscle must work.

2. Repetitions. This refers to the number of times each exercise is repeated in a single set, and to the number of sets.

3. Rate. This is the speed at which the exercises are performed.[38]

Once you understand these concepts, Table 10.1 can serve as a guideline in helping you to set up a program of exercises that will build speed as well as endurance into your muscles.

Table 10.1

|  | RESISTANCE | REPETITIONS | RATE |
|---|---|---|---|
| To build speed | High | Low | High |
| To build endurance | Low | High | High |

As far as determining more specifically how many repetitions you should do to build speed and how many to build endurance, use your ability as a guide. You can do this by making sure that the last one or two repetitions in a set are quite difficult, but not impossible for you. When all the repetitions in a set become fairly easy, increase the tension or weight you have been working with. Also, spend roughly twice the number of seconds doing endurance repetitions as you spend doing speed repetitions.

Before I go into specific training equipment, I'd like to say a short word about bulky muscles. If you're worried that the following exercises will significantly increase the size of your muscles, don't! Any exercises that you can do at high speed will not build bulk. Large muscles are slow muscles and only make swimming more difficult.

## INEXPENSIVE STRENGTH TRAINING EQUIPMENT (FOR USE AT HOME)

### Elastic Cords

From an 8 to 10 foot (about 3 meters) length of ½ inch (1.2 cm.) diameter surgical tubing, you can make a useful device by turning the ends back and fastening them with wire or tape to form handles. Wrap the center several times around a doorknob or other stationary object, hold on to the handles, bend at your waist to simulate a swimming position, and stand at a point where you can perform a complete swimming arm cycle without the cord becoming completely loose when your hands are all the way forward. You can increase the tension by stepping backward or by wrapping the cord one or two more times in the middle. Be sure to go through your full range of motion for each exercise. (You may wish to wear gloves to avoid blisters.)

1. Freestyle-butterfly drill. Simulate the arm action of the butterfly.
2. Breaststroke drill. Do the breaststroke arm pull.
3. Backstroke drill. Lying down on a bench or on the floor (a bench is better), pull both arms down simultaneously, following the backstroke pull pattern.
4. Lat Drill. Attach your cord to a hook in the ceiling and wrap the cord so that you can stand and pull your hands down (keeping your elbows high) from eye level to complete arm extension at the hips.
5. Kneeling lat drill. This is the same as number 4 only you kneel (to increase resistance).

### Pulleys

A pulley device is simply a rope with a handle at one end, a weight at the other end and a fixed pulley in the middle, so that when you grasp the handle, the rope forms a right angle and the weight or weights rest on the floor. Pulleys come in pairs: one for each arm; commercial models have interchangeable weights. You can make your own by using bricks or cans filled with concrete and one eye-bolt. For all but the backstroke drill, stand bent forward at the waist to simulate a swimming position.

1. Freestyle drill. Simulate the freestyle pull.
2. Breaststroke drill. Follow the breaststroke pull pattern.
3. Butterfly drill. Stroke as in butterfly.
4. Backstroke drill. Lie down on a bench or on the floor and simulate the backstroke pull.

### Exer-Genie

This is a commercially available device which operates on the principle of resistance caused by a friction rope. With an Exer-Genie, you can strengthen not just the arms, shoulders, and legs, but the entire body in a very small space. The device comes with a complete book of exercises for many different sports, including swimming, as well as general body strength. The cost of an Exer-Genie is about $35, and it mounts and dismounts easily between a door and its frame. (For more information, write to the address under

Exer-Genie in Appendix D.)

## Homemade Barbells

Barbells can be very inexpensive if you make them yourself from iron pipe and tin cans filled with concrete. Depending upon how much weight you need, use pipe that is from 1 to 2 inches (2.4 to 4.8 cm.) in diameter and about 4 feet (120 cm.) long, and use large cans (a 48 fluid ounce or 1.4 liter can will yield a barbell of approximately 21 pounds (about 9.5 kg.). Concrete, which can be purchased already mixed for easy use, should fill the pipe as well as the cans. Commercial barbells may also be used for the following exercises.

1.　Straight arm lift. Lie on your back, arms extended behind your head, holding the barbell with your hands shoulder width apart. Without bending your elbows, raise the barbell to a vertical position, then lower it.

2.　Bent arm lift. Lie on your back, arms bent to form right angles behind your head. Hold the barbell with your hands shoulder width apart, and without allowing your elbows to leave the floor, raise the barbell to a vertical position, then lower it.

3.　Elbow press. Stand or kneel, and with straight arms hold the barbell directly overhead, hands shoulder width apart or less. Keeping your elbows up, lower the barbell until it nearly touches the back of your neck, then raise the barbell.

4.　Wrist extension. Sit with your forearms resting on top of your thighs. Holding the barbell with your palms up, bend your wrists toward you as far as possible. Then allow your wrists to bend away from you as far as possible, by letting the barbell roll down your fingers. Return it to the starting position.

5.　Knee bends. Stand with the barbell resting on your shoulders behind your neck and your feet slightly apart, with one in front of the other. Keeping your body erect, bend your knees until your legs form approximately 45-degree angles. Then straighten your legs and, at last, rise up on your toes. Return to the starting position.

6.　Back lift. Stand with slightly bent knees and bend over so you can hold the barbell, palms facing backward, behind your calves. Keeping your elbows straight, raise the barbell until your arms are parallel to the floor, then lower the barbell.[39]

## Homemade Dumbbells

You can make dumbbells the same way you make barbells, only use a 1-foot (30 cm.) length of pipe and small size soup or vegetable cans. When you use dumbbells, you can do exercises that require you to move your arms in opposite directions at the same time. An example is for you to bend at your waist, allowing your arms to hang, holding the dumbbells, palms down; then raise the weights straight out to the sides as high as you can, and lower them. Try making up other exercises of your own.

### Bricks

You can also use one brick (or two tied together) in each hand to do the dumbbell exercises, or the barbell exercises if you are just beginning strength building and you do not require a great deal of resistance. You may, however, find that bricks are more difficult to handle than barbells.

## PROFESSIONAL STRENGTH TRAINING EQUIPMENT
## (TO WHICH YOU MAY HAVE ACCESS)

### Universal Gym

This is the name given to a system of stationary weights, as opposed to barbells, which are considered "free" weights. The type of physiological change that takes place in your muscles, however, is much the same whether you use stationary weights or free weights. But the Universal Gym has the following advantages over barbells: (1) You can adjust the resistance to suit your needs easily and without touching the weights. (2) You can do a greater variety of exercises. (3) You will be safer because stationary weights cannot fall on you. (4) Many people can exercise at once in a relatively small space.

The only disadvantages of a Univeral Gym are related to accessibility, in terms of cost and the amount of space the apparatus itself occupies. Because of these considerations you will need to locate a recreation facility, school, or fitness center that has a Universal Gym at which you can train. But if you train in one of these places, you will also probably be able to consult someone on the proper use of the apparatus. Once you are familiar with the equipment, try the following exercises:

1. Leg press.
2. Leg extension (sitting up).
3. Leg extension (lying on your stomach).
4. Sit-ups on an angle (knees bent).
5. Lat pull (elbows bent).
6. Tricep press-down.
7. Shoulder lift.
8. Dips.

9.   Tricep press (behind legs).
10.  Knee lift (from a hanging position).

(For more information, write to the address under Universal Gym in Appendix D.)

### Nautilus

Nautilus is the name of another type of equipment that makes use of stationary weights, but it is more sophisticated than the Universal Gym because of a "cam" device which is shaped like a nautilus shell, from which it derives its name. This cam allows the resistance which you encounter to vary with the degree of contraction of your muscles as you go through a particular range of motion. With ordinary weights you can only press or lift as much weight as the weakest area of your full range can tolerate, which means that during much of your range, the training benefit you gain is quite limited and you must therefore do many repetitions. With the Nautilus, on the other hand, you can tax a muscle fully throughout an exercise because resistance is highest at the muscle's strongest point and lowest at its weakest. So this training is far more efficient and fewer repetitions are required.

Nautilus is, however, the most costly, the most space-consuming, and therefore often the most inaccessible strength-training equipment. But perhaps you can find a health club or fitness center in your area that has the equipment if you are willing to pay an annual or monthly fee to use it. After all, I believe that Nautilus training is the best and most efficient way to build basic strength. I would suggest, though, that if you are serious about building swimming strength, you supplement your Nautilus program with some speed work using another device since Nautilus is not designed for high rate training. (For more information, write to the address under Nautilus in Appendix D.)

### Mini-Gym

Mini-Gym is the brand name for a whole line of exercise equipment in which the resistance adjusts automatically according to the force being applied by the muscles. This type of exercise apparatus is called "isokinetic," which refers to the applied principle that if the resistance working against a moving object (such as a hand) is exactly equal to the force exerted in the opposite direction, the object will continue to move at a constant speed.

I feel that Mini-Gym has the following advantages over other types of exercise equipment:

1.   It is designed specifically for swimming.
2.   It adjusts automatically to the strong and weak points of

the *individual* rather than to predetermined "normal" range-of-motion limitations.

3. It automatically adjusts to fatiguing muscles so it is virtually impossible to suffer injury from overtaxing a muscle.

4. A strong swimmer and a weak or even rehabilitation swimmer can exercise with the same device and receive the same training benefit without having to set any controls.

5. It is well-suited to high speed training.

6. It is less costly and less space consuming than other professional equipment.

(For more information, write to the address under Mini-Gym in Appendix D.)

No one training device can offer you as many benefits as several, despite the limitations of time, space, or money. But the positive approach to this situation is that many swimmers can do their dry-land training at one time through a series of stations with different devices (or with no device, such as a sit-up station or a stretching station). Such a series is called a "circuit," and in addition to being practical, it adds variety to your out-of-the-water program.

The following are some suggestions for consideration when using any strength training method:

1. Always make sure that you go through your full range of motion with any exercise.

2. Whenever possible, simulate the positions and movements you use in swimming.

3. Do some speed work and some endurance work.

4. Do many different exercises and create a circuit, even if you train alone.

5. While flexibility training should be done every day, heavy strength training should be limited to three times per week.

6. As you grow stronger, increase resistance rather than repetitions.

## IN-THE-WATER EXERCISES THAT BUILD STRENGTH

Although strength training in general is most efficiently done out of the water, because resistance can be more easily controlled, several in-the-water techniques are of value and can lend variety to your swimming workout.

### Vertical Kicking

Kicking with a breaststroke or "eggbeater" kick (kicking breaststroke one leg at a time) in a vertical position with your hands elevated above the surface or on top of your head is an excellent means of strengthening your legs at the same time as you increase your cardiovascular capacity. It is most beneficial to remain in a completely vertical position if you can, since leaning forward or backward allows your natural buoyancy to assist you.

The higher out of the water you can bring your body with the force of your kick, the greater the training benefit. My suggestion for a pattern of work and rest would be to kick for 30 seconds, then rest for 15 seconds and repeat for 3 minutes or more.

### Head-Out Freestyle

You should not attempt this exercise until you have good solid stroke mechanics in freestyle because, as you will recall, holding the head too high is a stroke defect. But as an exercise, swimming freestyle with your head out for short sprints can increase strength in your legs, since they must work harder to stay near the surface.

### Feet-First Breaststroke

To do this exercise, your body should be in a right angle position with your hips down in the water and your ankles and ears above the surface. Propulsion comes from taking small breaststroke pulls at your sides so that your body moves forward feet first.

According to Dave Scott, coach of the Davis Aquatic Masters and originator of the exercise, this is a good way to strengthen your abdominal muscles and your triceps.[40]

### Swimming in Place

Swimming without motion can be a useful method if you sometimes have access only to a very small swimming area, such as a motel or backyard pool. I would not, however, recommend that you do a large percentage of your swimming in this fashion because there are certain hydrodynamic differences between swimming through water that is not moving in relation to your body and water that is. You are, after all, training to improve your efficiency at moving forward.

To swim in place you will need an 18 to 20 foot (6 meters) length of ½ inch (1.2 cm.) diameter surgical tubing and a sturdy, preferably wide, canvas belt. Make a loop at each end of the tubing through which the belt can fit. Attach the middle of the tubing by wrapping it several times around a ladder, pole, or other stationary object near the edge of the pool. Slip the belt through the tubing loops and tighten the belt around your waist. Then swim out from the edge as far as the tubing will allow, and keep stroking to avoid slipping backward. Hold your position for a particular number of strokes or a certain length of time.

### Press-Ups

Begin by placing your hands, shoulder width apart, flat on the edge of the pool while allowing your body to rest in a vertical position in deep water. (If water deeper than your height isn't available, try bending your knees in this position in shallower water.) Then press your body up out of the water until your elbows are locked. Return to the starting position. You may wish to drape a towel over the edge of the pool to avoid abrasion to your wrists and rubbing the front of your suit.

Try doing press-ups in sets of ten or twenty at a time, or however many you can do without interrupting a continuous up and down motion. This will provide you with an excellent means of developing the strength necessary for a strong arm stroke finish in freestyle, backstroke, and butterfly. Also, remember to press out of the pool whenever possible, rather than using a ladder as you leave the water. Press-ups should, however, be discontinued if any wrist pain develops.

## OTHER SPORTS THAT CONTRIBUTE TO GOOD SWIMMING

Any sport that raises heart rate to 60 percent of maximum or more for a period of at least 20 minutes and is performed regularly will induce an excellent cardiovascular training benefit that is useful in swimming. Clearly, if you are capable of maintaining high heart rate during one activity, you will be better able to maintain it during others. But in relation to cardiovascular fitness, the problem with many sports which depend upon rules or are played as a game, such as tennis, basketball, or soccer is that heart rate goes up and down rapidly. And the best contributors to fitness are those activities that permit a *constantly* increased heart rate. Examples of such sports are swimming, running, cycling, and rowing.

The other element, as you have seen in this chapter, that contributes to good swimming is specific muscular strength, which to a much higher degree comes from doing swimming-like exercises than from playing terrestrial sports. But please do not take this to mean that you should avoid taking a break from swimming for a few months to participate in another sport. You may well find the variety exciting. And remember, muscles (with some use, that is) lose their strength far less rapidly than your heart and lungs lose their state of fitness.

## CHAPTER SUMMARY:

Flexibility and strength training should supplement rather than substitute for your swimming, whenever possible.

Stretching to gain flexibility is an easy activity to add to your day because it can be done anytime, anywhere.

Flexibility is the range of motion of a joint.

Flexibility is the foundation of all movement.

Stretch before and after exercise, and any other time you like.

Stretching can relieve aches and pains.

### Stretching Exercises

Shoulders

1.  Forward arm circles.
2.  Backward arm circles.
3.  Forward and back arm swings.
4.  Partner arm stretches.
5.  Chicken wings.
6.  "N" stretches.
7.  Arms-over-head stretches.
8.  Towel stretches.

Legs and Ankles

1.  Toe touches.
2.  Plantar sits.
3.  Push-ups on the wall.
4.  Hurdle stretches.
5.  Breaststroke squats.
6.  Rocker squats.
7.  Yoga sits.

Spine and Abdomen

1.  Back stretchers.
2.  Front extensions.
3.  Airplane twists.
4.  Rolls back and forth.
5.  Side stretches.
6.  Speed skaters.
7.  Jackknife sit-ups.
8.  Plantar push-ups.
9.  Heel raisers.

Strength training equipment can be very inexpensive or very expensive, and some strength training requires no equipment at all.

In general, exercises using inexpensive equipment and no equipment build nonspecific strength, while exercises using expensive equipment build specific strength.

"Static" strength building requires muscles to exert force which results in little or no movement.

"Dynamic" strength building requires the muscles to

exert force through the entire range of motion of a joint.

Isometric exercises increase strength without motion and without equipment.

## Isometric Exercises

1. Arm press-up with straight arms.
2. Arm press-up with bent arms.
3. Wall press.
4. Leg lift.
5. Ankle press-up.
6. Table press-up.
7. Table press-down.
8. Doorway press.

Dynamic strength training relates better to swimming because both involve a full range of motion.

The "Three R's of Exercise" are resistance, repetitions, and rate.

To build speed into your muscles you need high resistance, low repetitions, and high rate.

To build endurance you need low resistance, high repetitions, and high rate.

Use your ability as a guide to determining how many repetitions and how much weight to work with.

## Inexpensive Strength Training Equipment

### Elastic cords

1. Freestyle-butterfly drill.
2. Breaststroke drill.
3. Backstroke drill.
4. Lat drill.
5. Kneeling lat drill.

### Pulleys

1. Freestyle drill.
2. Breaststroke drill.
3. Butterfly drill.
4. Backstroke drill.

### Exer-Genie

### Homemade barbells

1. Straight arm lift.
2. Bent arm lift.
3. Elbow press.
4. Wrist extension.
5. Knee bends.
6. Back lift.

Homemade Dumbbells

Bricks

### Professional Strength Training Equipment

Universal Gym

1. Leg press.
2. Leg extension (sitting up).
3. Leg extension (lying on your stomach).
4. Sit-ups on an angle (knees bent).
5. Lat pull (elbows bent).
6. Tricep pressdown.
7. Shoulder lift.
8. Dips.
9. Tricep press (behind legs).
10. Knee lift (from a hanging position).

Nautilus

Mini-Gym

### In-the-Water Exercises that Build Strength

1. Vertical kicking.
2. Head-out freestyle.
3. Feet-first breaststroke.
4. Swimming in place.

5. Press-ups.

### Other Sports that Contribute to Good Swimming

Sports which maintain a continuously high heart rate, such as running, cycling, and rowing induce an excellent cardiovascular training benefit that is useful in swimming.

# 11. *Your First Swimming Season*

*I*f you have followed with some regularity even a fraction of the suggestions in this book, you probably are already a successful swimmer. You have achieved something that many people consider to be nearly impossible, and the time has certainly come to give yourself a well-deserved pat on the back. After all, *you* turned a lot of words into a successful swimming experience for yourself.

Perhaps, also, you have been feeling pretty good in general and you have been enjoying your training. Or maybe things haven't been going so well for you, and your time in the water has provided a welcome diversion from your unsettling affairs. In either case — and if you've been swimming any time at all, you've probably experienced both — your swimming plays a role whose importance should not be overlooked, even when progress is slower than you would like it to be. Remember, it is your *effort*, not your achievements that lead you to fitness and health.

But in being a successful swimmer, it may have occurred to you to put a little icing on the cake by giving competition a try. After all, it is a quite natural tendency once you are doing well to want to put yourself in a situation which could bring out your very best performance. And the Masters program has made it possible for adults of any age to compete.

One woman who certainly experiences the thrill of accomplishment through participation in competition is sixty-one-year-old Pat Matthiesen. During the 1978 Masters National Championships, she said, "It's exciting for me to go to a meet, enter an event and find I can finish. At first I was happy just to make 50 yards. Then I kept improving to 100 yards and 200 yards. I swam in the Nationals at Santa Monica in 1973 and entered the 200 yard freestyle, but after 150 yards, I had to start doing breaststroke. Then the very next year in Fort Lauderdale, I entered the 1650 yard freestyle and placed second."

Another woman with whom I talked several years ago, shortly after the skin-hugging lycra racing suits came on the market, was sixty-seven-year-old Sylvia Bailey who stood before me toweling off her firm, slim body and looking at least twenty years younger. She chatted with me about her training and meets to come when I noticed that she kept massaging one of her fingers. I asked if she had hurt herself and she replied with a thoughtful look, "Well, the truth of the matter is, I think I tore a ligament putting on my Belgrad [a brand of skin suit]."

Whether you are serious enough about swimming to compete in the 1650, or to wear a Belgrad in a race, though, competition will certainly provide an opportunity to increase your awareness of your own swimming and to highlight your strengths and weaknesses. Competition also lets you extend your personal limitations, whether your goal is to make a certain distance, to see if a particular training technique has paid off, or to experience the satisfaction of exerting yourself to the utmost. A teammate of mine, Jerry Smith, who competes in the 45 to 49-year age bracket, and who, incidentally, suffered a heart attack before starting to swim, thoroughly enjoys competition. As he says, "It works better for me to approach my race with a sense of wonder rather than fear, and to take a journey inside myself as I swim it, in much the same way that one would walk into a boiler room and examine all the gauges to see how the machinery is functioning. All of my interest is internalized; therefore I don't experience fear, but curiosity instead. And this helps to keep me in a state of harmony inside and out, and I'm free to do the best I can."

No matter how you approach the race or what your goals or reasons for competing are, the important thing is that you must not forget, once the eagerness to excel strikes, that fitness, health, and a sense of well-being are the real rewards of any swimming program and that everything else is really dessert. Since most of us do not have Jerry Smith's control over our feelings before and during a race, this statement bears remembering all the more.

Most of us have felt intimidated by the prospect of competition and have doubted the adequacy of our training the moment when we are standing on the starting block before a race, or even when we just imagine it. This feeling is difficult to avoid, but with some planning it can be minimized. It's important to realize, if you're already a competitor, that although your success as a swimmer does not depend upon the times you do or what place you come in; you can probably improve both and enhance your satisfaction with swimming at the same time. If you're not yet a competitor but have considered it, you should know that once the feeling of doubt hits you when you're standing on the starting block, it will be a comfort for you to know that you've planned ahead.

With this in mind, let's begin making a plan by focusing on forty-three-year-old Shirley Anderson, a wife, mother of two, legal secretary, and swimmer all in one. On the recommendation of a friend, she joined the local Masters swimming group that trains in the evenings and on Saturdays, but due to the many demands on her time, she's often unable to attend these sessions. Shirley therefore supplements her group training by swimming on her own whenever she can during the noon adult recreation swim. Between the two she has been averaging three or four workouts per week for most of the nine months since she joined the Masters.

During the first weeks of her training she was unable to swim more than two or three lengths at a time without stopping for 1 to 2 minutes to rest. After four months of swimming, Shirley was able to follow the posted workouts and complete all of the assignments except those that included large amounts of butterfly. And at about this time, at the recommendation of her coach, she started writing down the workouts she did, so that she would have something to go by on the days that she swam by herself and so that she could see her progress.

A typical page in her log book from her fifth month of training looks like this:

Swim 300 meters choice
of strokes warmup

| Swim 4 × 150 meters (leaving every 3:15) | 1st 50 — back |
| | 2nd 50 — breast |
| | 3rd 50 — free |
| | |
| Swim 4 × 150 meters free (leaving every 3 min.) | 1st 50 — feel stroke |
| | 2nd 50 — medium |
| | 3rd 50 — hard |
| | |
| Kick | :45 hard, :15 moderate |
| 2 × | :30 hard, :15 moderate |
| | :15 hard, :15 moderate |

Swim 4 × 25 meters sprint,
one each stroke (leaving
every :45)
Swim 200 meters swim-down
_____
1,900 meters total
+3 min. kicking

Two days later, she did this workout:

| Swim | 25 meters, 1st favorite stroke | |
| | 50 meters, 2nd favorite stroke | |
| | 75 meters, 3rd favorite stroke | warmup |

100 meters, 4th favorite stroke

| | |
|---|---|
| Swim 4 × 125 meters individual medley (leaving every 2:30) | #1 — 50 fly, 25 back, 25 breast, 25 free |
| | #2 — 25 fly, 50 back, 25 breast, 25 free |
| | #3 — 25 fly, 25 back, 50 breast, 25 free |
| | #4 — 25 fly, 25 back, 25 breast, 50 free |
| Kick 4 × 75 meters w/fins (leaving every 2:00) | 1st 25 — fly |
| | 2nd 25 — back |
| | 3rd 25 — free |
| Pull 4 × 75 meters free w/paddles & pull buoy (leaving every 1:45) | 1st 25 — breathe every 2 strokes |
| | 2nd 25 — breathe every 3 strokes |
| | 3rd 25 — breathe every 4 strokes |
| Swim 300 meters free | every 3rd 25 hard |
| Swim 4 × 50 meters sprint (leaving every 1:10) | one each stroke |
| Swim 100 meters swim-down | |

1,950 meters total

During the following six months of training, Shirley's endurance and stroke technique improved, particularly in butterfly, but she also reached that somewhat frustrating point where her improvement from day to day and even from one week to the next, was not so evident as it had been in the beginning. And she caught herself feeling annoyed for the first time one afternoon when a co-worker, glancing at Shirley's damp hair in passing, remarked, "I don't know why you put yourself through it."

One year later, when she trained with the Masters, Shirley was just beginning to swim in another lane of the pool with some of the more experienced swimmers. "What am I doing here?" she asked herself ten times a day, but as she began to form strong friendships with the others in her lane, she gave up the idea of going back where she came from. Besides, some of these friends were competitors and she felt she was learning from them. For example, she noted that they paid quite close attention to the clock, took very short rest periods, did mostly flip turns during freestyle and backstroke, and sometimes practiced racing dives near the end of practice.

A workout from this stage of Shirley's training is as follows:

Kick 200 meters

| | |
|---|---|
| Pull 200 meters | warmup |
| Swim 200 meters | |
| Kick & Swim 400 meters individual medley, kick a 50, swim a 50 of each stroke (rest :10 at each 50) | |
| Swim 20 × 50 meters | 5 breast (leaving every 1:10) |
| | 5 fly (leaving every 1:05) |
| | 5 back (leaving every 1:00) |
| | 5 free (leaving every :55) |
| Pull 100 meters easy free, very long strokes | |
| Swim 4 × 25 meters choice of strokes, very fast, from a dive (leaving every 1:00) | |
| Swim 200 meters swim-down | |

2,400 meters total

After this workout, Shirley felt a little disappointed that she was unable to make the intervals on all of the twenty 50s. "I had to sit out the second and fourth 50s of butterfly and the third 50 of backstroke," she told her coach, who immediately responded, "But you made all of the breast-stroke, and all of the last seven 50s, which really are the hardest." He continued to explain to her that since some of the swimmers would be going to the National Championships in three months, he was presently putting the team through "mid-season" training of which short rest intervals, high-intensity swimming, and increased total distance per work-out are typical. "So there's no reason to feel bad," he added, "if you're having a harder time than you were a month ago during the early season, when we were doing a lot of long, relaxed swims, heavy stroke work, and un-timed swimming."

A whole swimming "season" was something Shirley had not thought about before, but when she went back and looked through her log book, she realized, after scolding herself for not writing down her workouts more regularly, that there had indeed been a change in the format of her workouts in the last month. She recalled that a couple of months before she had been doing a great many odd dis-tance swims, such as 150s, 175s, 250s, each stressing a particular swimming skill, a stroke drill, or a variation in speed. "Well," she thought, closing her book with a slap, "what's it all to me? I'm certainly not going to the Na-tionals!" And yet somewhere in the deepest part of her was a tiny flicker of curiosity about what it would be like to swim in a race — not in the Nationals, of course, but just a race.

She forgot about the idea, though, for another couple of

months and continued as usual with her training until one day three of her teammates, one of whom was a very good friend and had originally talked Shirley into joining the Masters, asked if she would consider swimming with them in a relay at a nearby meet the following weekend. "Me? But I've never competed before!" was all she could think to say at first. And then she thought about the fact that the whole family was supposed to have an early dinner at her mother's house that day, and that she had to make lasagna for a potluck the next day. And what did she want to swim in a meet for anyway. And she'd slow down the relay for the others.

"No," she told them. "I can't possibly do it." But all the way home she thought about it. And she thought about the excitement over the Nationals that had been in the air at practice lately even though only a relatively small number of swimmers were going. There seemed to be positive vibrations coming from nearly everyone. And she herself was feeling quite strong on the program of longer rest, higher quality swimming, and shorter total distance per workout. That evening she had done the following practice:

Swim 400 meters choice of strokes, warm-up

Swim 4 × 100 meters free, every other length hard, work turns (leaving every 2:15)

Swim 200 meters individual medley, rest: 10 after each 50, very fast

200 meters your best stroke, rest :10 after each 50, very fast

Swim 200 meters easy

Swim Free   75 meters on 1:45, moderate
        2 × 50 meters on 1:15, fast
        25 meters, very fast

Practice turns

Swim 4 × 25 meters sprint choice of strokes, dive (leaving every 1:00)

Swim 200 meters swim-down

2,000 meters total

Although Shirley rarely discussed her swimming with the family for fear she'd never stop talking, this particular evening she just had to tell them that at practice some friends had asked her to go to a meet with them. Her husband beamed at her, but before he could say anything, her twelve-year-old spoke up. "You sure you're not too old to race, Mom?" he asked.

Her mind was made up. The next day she couldn't go to practice because she had to work late, but she phoned her friends to tell them that she had thought the matter over carefully and had decided she wanted to go to the meet after all. It was agreed. They would pick her up at 7:30 AM.

Shirley awoke long before her alarm the morning of the meet. For most of the night her bed had felt as if she'd never slept in it before. She dozed and woke again, still a quarter of an hour before the alarm.

The object now was to get ready and go without waking anyone. She felt an obsession not to draw attention to herself, but just to go on her way unnoticed and unmissed. And despite the tightness in her stomach, she smiled to herself at the prospect of going off with her friends for the day and leaving family responsibilities behind. "It's sort of like when I first learned to drive," she thought, swallowing her toast with some difficulty. The knot in her stomach was determined to stay with her.

After a good deal of giddy conversation and laughter on the way to the meet, Shirley felt suddenly alone, although her friends were still beside her, as she walked onto the pool deck and realized that this was where she would be swimming. A wave of butterflies exploded through her. But this feeling soon gave way to quite another. Her perceptions slowly moved outside of her physical self, away from the taut feeling in her stomach and away from a vaguely formed, only partially conscious feeling that somehow the entire course of human events was about to be altered because *she*

was going to dive in and swim a race. There seemed to be thousands of swimmers around her, although in reality there were maybe 150, all with an aura of vigor and vitality about them, and most with an air of exhilaration over the sheer joy of the moment. Young and old alike, side by side — some doing stretching exercises on the deck, some conversing with teammates, some trying out the starting blocks or loosening up in the pool — seemed to revel in being exactly where they were at exactly that moment.

"Shirley," called one of the members of her team, "it's great to see you here! Come put your things down with the rest of us."

Shirley gladly followed, only to be nearly knocked over by Nancy, one of the relay team members, who excitedly showed Shirley in the meet program that only five swimmers from Shirley's age group were entered in the 100-yard freestyle event. "I'm in it," said Nancy, "and I think you should swim it with me."

Before Shirley knew it she and Nancy were at the Clerk of the Course filling out Shirley's card for the 100 free. "What about my time?" Shirley asked.

"Use your practice time," said Nancy.

"And I don't have an AAU number yet. I've only just applied for my card."

"Put down 'applied for' next to the space for AAU number," said Nancy smiling and patting Shirley's arm. "You'll do fine, I just know it."

During her warmup Shirley had some trouble really loosening up and she thought that her strokes felt odd. But getting in the water did ease her nerves and after about 500 yards of slow swimming she felt looser than she had when she first got in. She then did two or three fast sprints from the blocks and then got out of the pool.

The women's 100 yard free was event number 11 so Shirley had some time to watch a lot of the other swimmers do their events before it was her turn. The highlight of her observation came when she saw a little boy of about seven rush up to the edge of the pool during the women's 50 yard backstroke and yell impatiently, "Go, grandma, go!"

When Shirley's turn came, she was beginning to wonder if standing on the block without having to go to the bathroom for the fourteenth time wouldn't be the hardest part. But as she stood before the pool, seeing several of her teammates waving at her from the other end, she felt that she had come a long way with them and that she and they and in a sense all of the swimmers at the meet were one in their training, their camaraderie, and most of all in their appreciation of supreme physical effort.

The race went by like a blur for Shirley. Suddenly it was over. She couldn't recall having thought about anything while she was swimming, but somehow, through her own movement, she supposed, she had landed in the water and managed to swim four lengths of the pool.

She was so glad it was over, and even through the web of her exhaustion a feeling of pride for what she had done was spreading. Her teammates were jumping up and down telling her she had placed third.

Later as she talked to her coach about the race and looked at the time for the first 50 yards as compared to the time for the second 50, she began to recollect a few of the details of the race and they talked about how she could improve next time. "On the relay, try not to get so close to the wall on your turn," he said.

She was to swim second on the relay and was very nervous about not losing any of the ground that the first swimmer gave her. This time she tried to give herself a little more room at the wall for her turn. Then the second length, she gave it all she had even when she started to feel that each stroke would be the last of her life. Someone helped her drag herself out of the pool at the end, but as the fourth swimmer on the relay was coming in for the finish, she found herself jumping up and down with the others.

"It was a glorious race," chanted Shirley that evening to anyone at her mother's house who would listen. "And we all clung to each other at the end like exhausted children after a tug-of-war," she continued, showing her second and third place ribbons.

"Shirley," said her brother-in-law, who had silently listened to her entire account, "I've been thinking a lot about fitness lately. How can I get started swimming?"

# *Footnotes*

1. Paul Hutinger, "Physiological Advantages of Training with Swimming," *Masters Swimmers Lane 4* 2 (Sept.-Oct. 1978): 2.

2. Joyce Brothers, *Better Than Ever* (New York: Dell Publishing Co., 1977), 37.

3. Hal Higdon, *Fitness After Forty* (Mtn. View: World Publications, 1977), p. 225.

4. Paul Hutinger, "The Stress of Swimming," *Aquatic World* (Sept. 1974): 23.

5. Paul Hutinger, "The Fountain of Youth," *Aquatic World* (Nov. 1974): 20.

6. Hutinger, "The Stress of Swimming," p. 23.

7. Herbert A. deVries, *Physiology of Exercise for Physical Education* (Philadelphia: W. B. Saunders Co., 1976), p. 111.

8. Paul Hutinger, "Advice for the Swimmer's Body," *Aquatic World* (Jan. 1976): 29.

9. Hutinger [quoting Forbes Carlile], "Advice for the Swimmer's Body," p. 29.

10. Dick Hannula, "A Catalog of Swimming Drills," *Swimming Technique* 10 (July 1973): 34-35.

11. James E. Counsilman, *Competitive Swimming Manual for Coaches and Swimmers* (Bloomington: Counsilman Co., Inc., 1977), p. 6.

12. *Ibid.*, p. 7.

13. *Ibid.*, p. 87.

14. *Ibid.*, p. 3.

15. *Ibid.*, p. 87-88.

16. Counsilman, "Hypoxic and Other Methods of Training Evaluated," handout material at the American Swimming Coaches' Association Clinic, Dec. 5-7, 1974, at Las Vegas.

17. *Ibid.*, p. 2.

18. *Ibid.*, p. 2-3.

19. Don Schwartz, "Stroke Instruction/Analysis for Freestyle and Butterfly," presentation at the Tamalpais Masters Swim Clinic, Dec. 10, 1977, at Kentfield, California.

20. Anthony Power, "Swimming Injuries: Their Causes, Treatment, and Prevention," *Swimming Coach* 76 (Winter 1976): 15.

21. *Ibid.*

22. Patsi Sinnott, a conversation with the author, April 16, 1978, Davis, Calif.

23. Nancy Ridout, "Relief for Shoulder Pain or Tendonitis," *Swim-Master* 6 (May 1977): 1.

24. Stuart A. Bergman, Jr., "Cardiovascular Aspects of Training vs. Overtraining," *Track and Field Quarterly Review* (Dec. 1974): 6. p. 6.

25. Hutinger, "The Stress of Swimming," p. 23.

26. deVries, p. 500.

27. Paul Hutinger, "Hints for Masters," *Aquatic World* (July 1975): 26.

28.   Jill Kelly, Jane Leavy, Ann Northrop, "Who Says Athletes Can't Be Pregnant?" *Ms.* 7 (July 1978): 48.

29.   *Ibid.*, p. 48.

30.   Harold Dennis supplied this information in a telephone conversation with the author on Sept. 29, 1978, San Bruno, Calif.

31.   Kelly, Leavy, and Northrop, p. 48.

32.   Counsilman, *Competitive Swimming Manual for Coaches and Swimmers*, p. 125.

33.   Robert Anderson, *Stretching* (Fullerton: Stretching, P.O. Box 2734, Fullerton, Calif., 1978) p. 4.

34.   *Ibid.*, p. 111.

35.   *Ibid.*, p. 112.

36.   *Ibid.*, p. 111.

37.   Counsilman, "The Importance of Speed in Exercise," *The Athletic Journal* (May 1976): 73-74.

38.   *Ibid.*, p. 72.

39.   Counsilman, *Competitive Swimming Manual for Coaches and Swimmers*, p. 116.

40.   David Scott, a conversation with the author, Dec. 17, 1977, Davis, Calif.

41.   Hutinger, "The Fountain of Youth," *Aquatic World* (Nov. 1974): 19-20.

# *Bibliography*

Amateur Athletic Union of the United States. *Amateur Athletic Union Code Handbook*. Indianapolis: 1978.

Anderson, R. A. *Stretching*. Fullerton: Stretching, P.O. Box 2734, Fullerton, Calif. 92633, 1978.

Armbruster, D. A., Allen, R. H., and Billingsley, H. S. *Swimming and Diving*. 6th ed., St. Louis: The C. V. Mosby Co., 1973.

Bergman, S. A., Jr. "Cardiovascular Aspects of Training vs. Overtraining." *Track and Field Quarterly Review* (Dec. 1974).

Brothers, J. *Better Than Ever*. New York: Dell Publishing Co., Inc. 1977. (Abridged from: *Better Than Ever* by Joyce Brothers. New York: Simon & Schuster, Inc., 1975).

Caldwell, F. "The Search for Strength." *Swimming Technique* 15 (Summer 1978): 49-51.

Chalip, L. "Tethered Swimming Reconsidered." *Swimming Technique* 15 (Spring 1978): 13-14.

Colwin, C. "Butterfly for Beginners." *Swimming World and Junior Swimmer* 19 (Feb. 1978): 8-13.

———. *An Introduction to Swimming Coaching*. Toronto: Canadian Amateur Swimming Assoc., 1977.

Counsilman, J. E. *Competitive Swimming Manual for Coaches and Swimmers*. Bloomington: Counsilman Co., Inc., 1977.

———. "Hypoxic and Other Methods of Training Evaluated." Copy of hand-out material at the American Swimming Coaches' Assoc. Clinic, Dec. 5-7, 1974, at Las Vegas, Nev.

———. "The Importance of Speed in Exercise." *The Athletic Journal* (May 1976): 72-74.

deVries, H. A. *Physiology of Exercise for Physical Education*. Philadelphia: W. B. Saunders Co., 1976.

Hannula, D. "A Catalog of Swimming Drills." *Swimming Technique* 10 (July 1973): 34-38.

Higdon, H. *Fitness after Forty*. Mountain View: World Publications, 1977.

Hutinger, P. "Advice for the Swimmer's Body." *Aquatic World* (Jan. 1976): 28.

———. "The Fountain of Youth." *Aquatic World* (Nov. 1974): 18-21.

———. "Hints for Masters." *Aquatic World* (July 1975): 26-28.

———. "Physiological Advantages of Training with Swimming." *Masters Swimmers Lane 4* 2 (Sept.-Oct. 1978): 2.

———. "Pumping You through Your Laps." *Aquatic World* (Jan. 1975): 22-24.

———. "The Stress of Swimming." *Aquatic World* (Sept. 1974): 22-23.

———. "Training Techniques for Masters Swimmers." Reprinted from the 1973 Long Course Masters' National Championship Program, Chicago.

"Hypoxic Training — The Czech System." *Sports & Fitness Instructor* (March 1973).

Jensen, Clayne, and Jensen, Craig. "Update on Strength Training."

*Scholastic Coach* (May/June 1977).

Kelly, J., Leavy, J., and Northrop, A. "Who Says Athletes Can't be Pregnant?" *Ms.* VII (July 1978): 47-48.

Pipes, T. V. "Strength-Training Modes: What's the Difference?" *Scholastic Coach* (May/June 1977).

Power, A. "Swimming Injuries: Their Causes, Treatment, and Prevention." The British Swimming Coaches' Bulletin: *Swimming Coach* 76 (Winter 1976): 15-21.

Reynolds, B. "Sensible Weight Training." *Aquatic World* (March 1976): 10-12.

Ridout, N. "Relief for Shoulder Pain or Tendonitis." *Swim-Master* VI (May 1977): 1.

Scheihauf, B. "A Hydrodynamic Analysis of Breaststroke Pulling Proficiency." *Swimming Technique* 12 (Winter 1976): 100-105.

Schwartz, D. "Stroke Instruction/Analysis for Freestyle and Butterfly." Presentation at the Tamalapis Masters Swim Clinic, Dec. 10, 1977 at Kentfield, Calif.

Spitz, M., and LeMond, A. *The Mark Spitz Complete Book of Swimming.* New York: Thomas Y. Crowell Co., 1976.

"Old Sternwheeler's." *Swim-Master* VI (Sept. 1977): 3.

# *Appendix A*

## SOURCES OF INFORMATION ON MASTERS SWIMMING PROGRAMS IN THE UNITED STATES

Because of the very large number of Masters swimming programs in existence in the United States and the speed with which new clubs are organizing, I found it difficult to provide anything near a complete and up-to-date list of Masters swimming groups. Probably the best way to find out what competitive teams there are in a certain area is to call or write the following address:

United State Masters Swimming
c/o Dorothy Donnelly
5 Piggott Lane
Avon
Connecticut 06001
(203) 677-9464

Also, *Swim Swim* Magazine, a publication for adult fitness and competitive swimmers has a section entitled "Places to Swim" which lists Masters clubs as well as fitness swimming locations.

*Swim Swim* Magazine
8461 Warner Drive
Culver City
California 90230
(213) 558-3321

Other good sources of information on adult fitness swimming programs, adult lap swimming sessions, as well as Masters swimming schedules, are city and county recreation departments, park departments, park districts, YMCAs, YWCAs, schools, independent recreation centers, swimming clubs, and public swimming pools.

# *Appendix B*

## A SAMPLE HEALTH INFORMATION FORM

It is an excellent idea for any Masters team or organized group of swimmers to maintain an up-to-date file of health information cards on all swimmers in the group. Each card should provide emergency telephone numbers for each swimmer as well as pertinent health data such as a history of diabetes, epilepsy, arthritis, heart trouble, or any other condition to which the coach or supervisor of the group should be alerted. The Davis Aquatic Masters of Davis, California, use this health survey form. The information it asks for is vital to anyone who must effectively handle on-the-spot health problems and should be provided by each swimmer as soon as he or she joins the group.

### HEALTH QUESTIONNAIRE
### DAVIS AQUATIC MASTERS

Name: _____Age: _____ Date: _____

In case of emergency contact: _____

Address: _____

Phone: _____

1. Do you have any medical or surgical illnesses or conditions?

   List: _____

2. Do you take any medications? List: _____

   _____

3. Do you have any allergies? List: _____

   Are you allergic to any medication? List: _____

   _____

4. Have you ever had:   rheumatic fever _____

                        heart murmur _____

                        real or suspected heart attack _____

                        chest pains _____

                        coronary occlusions _____

                        irregular heart beat _____

valve replacement _____

5. Do you have high blood pressure? _____

6. Do you have diabetes (high sugar level in the blood or urine)?

_____

7. Have you ever had an electrocardiogram (EKG) which was ab-

normal? _____

8. Do you have any lung illnesses (asthma, emphysema, bronchitis,

etc.)? _____

9. Has a doctor ever ordered you to limit your physical activity?

Explain: _____

10. Do you have any other physical limitations or medical problems?

List: _____

_____

# *Appendix C*

## SOME PHYSIOLOGICAL CHANGES
## THAT RESULTED FROM EXERCISE

These data are from one of the very few long-term studies on Masters swimming which is currently being conducted at Western Illinois University. Before the study began the subject, Paul Hutinger, was 46 years old and had trained two months a year, five days a week, so he was at a better-than-average level of fitness. At age 49, he began a year-round training program consisting of 2000 yards a day, six days a week of interval training. The study yielded the following results:

1.    Reduced blood pressure.

| Age 46 | Age 49 | Male Average for age 49 |
|---|---|---|
| 126/85 mm Hg | 115/75 mm Hg | 140/85 mm Hg |

While not all people respond to exercise with reduced blood pressure, many do and they reduce the risk of heart disease.

2.    Lower resting pulse rate.

| Age 46 | Age 49 | Male Average for age 49 |
|---|---|---|
| 62 bpm* | 53 bpm | 72 bpm |

*beats per minute

A lower resting pulse rate decreases the risk of heart disease because the heart can carry on its necessary function with less strain.

3.    Improved maximum breathing capacity.

| Age 46 | Age 49 | Male Average for age 49 |
|---|---|---|
| 140 l/min. | 117 l/min. | 110 l/min. |

Maximum breathing capacity is measured by the amount of air (in litres) that a person can inhale in one minute.

4.    Improved oxygen uptake.

| Age 46 | Age 49 | Male Average for age 49 |
|---|---|---|
| 50 ml/kg/min | 56 ml/kg/min | 38 ml/kg/min |

Oxygen uptake is measured by the amount of oxygen the body can deliver to the muscles and organs. Physical work capacity means the same as oxygen uptake. It is usually measured by working the subject to his maximum effort on some device such as a treadmill or a bicycle ergometer which can exactly measure the effort exerted. (By comparison, it is interesting to note that in a fitness standards study on male college students done in 1973 by Dr. E. G. Fox, the average was found to be 41-48 ml/kg/min.)

5.    Reduced percentage of body fat.

| Age 46 | Age 49 | Male Average for age 49 |
|---|---|---|
| 12.2 percent | 11.8 percent | 20 percent |

Body fat can be measured by the skin fold test, or, more exactly by underwater weighing. Exercise changes body composition but weight in regard to body fat is determined by the amount of food intake in relation to work output.

6.    Improved cholesterol level.

| Age 46 | Age 49 | Male Average for age 49 |
|---|---|---|
| 232 mg/100ml | 210 mg/100ml | 250 mg/100ml |

Cholesterol is a lipid substance that accumulates with age inside the blood vessels and is associated with cardiovascular diseases. Exercise and diet are very important in controlling cholesterol levels.

7.  Greater blood volume.

| Age 46 | Age 49 | Male Average for age 49 |
|---|---|---|
| 5 litres | 6 litres | 5 litres |

Blood volume does depend on the size of the individual, but, in any case, blood volume will increase with regular aerobic exercise. This, in turn, enables more oxygen to be delivered to body tissues. On the average, a male who is 5'7" and weighs 150 lbs. will have 5 litres of blood.

8.  Increased hemoglobin level.

| Age 46 | Age 49 | Male Average for age 49 |
|---|---|---|
| 14.7 g/100cc | 15.7 g/100cc | 13-17 g/100cc |

Hemoglobin is the protein in red blood cells which combines with oxygen and is directly related to the oxygen carrying capacity of the blood.

9.  Higher hematocrit level.

| Age 46 | Age 49 | Male Average for age 49 |
|---|---|---|
| 44.5 percent | 48.6 percent | 40-50 percent |

Hematocrit level is the percentage of red blood cells in whole blood which is also directly related to the oxygen-carrying capacity of the blood.

10.  Greater functional ability of the heart.

| Age 46 | Age 49 | Male Average for age 49 |
|---|---|---|
| Heart rate 182 at maximum capacity | Heart rate 180 at maximum capacity | |

The functional ability of the heart refers to heart efficiency. So if maximum capacity remains nearly constant, attaining maximum capacity with a lower heart rate demonstrates a higher level of heart stroke efficiency.[47]

The important idea to bear in mind when considering these results, is that any person (no matter what his age or his present level of conditioning) who is physically capable of swimming can reap at least to some degree the same benefits as the subject in this study if his training is regular.

# Appendix D

## SOURCES OF INFORMATION
## ON STRENGTH-BUILDING EQUIPMENT

1. Exer-Genie, Inc.
P.O. Box 3320
Fullerton,
California 92634

2. Universal Gym
Centurion Sales Company
P.O. Box P
Mountain View,
California 94042

3. Nautilus Sports/Medical
Industries
P.O. Box 1783
Deland, Florida 32720

4. Mini-Gym, Inc.
P.O. Box 266
909 W. Lexington
Independence,
Missouri 64051